WILLIAM GOLDING

LITERATURE AND LIFE: BRITISH WRITERS
Select list of titles in the series:

Complete list of titles in the series available from the publisher on request

WILLIAM GOLDING

Lawrence S. Friedman

A Frederick Ungar Book
CONTINUUM • NEW YORK

1993

The Continuum Publishing Company
370 Lexington Avenue, New York, NY 10017

Printed in the United States of America

Library of Congress Cataloging-in-Publication Data

Friedman, Lawrence S.
    William Golding / Lawrence S. Friedman.
        p.   cm. — (Literature and life. British writers)
    "A Frederick Ungar book."
    Includes bibliographical references and index.
    ISBN 0-8264-0564-9 (cloth)
        1. Golding, William, 1911–   .   2. Novelists, English—20th
    century—Biography.   I. Title.   II. Series.
    PR6013.035Z63   1993
    823'.914—dc20
    [B]   91-41115
                                                                      CIP

Contents

Chronology

1911   September 19, William Golding is born at St. Col-
        umb Manor, Cornwall, the son of Alec Golding,
        a mathematics teacher and senior master of Marl-
        borough Grammar School, and Mildred Golding,
        an early suffragette.

1930   After completing his secondary schooling at the
        Marlborough School, Golding enters Brasenose
        College, Oxford, to read science before switching
        to literature two years later.

1934   *Poems*, Golding's first book, is published in Mac-
        millan's Contemporary Poets series.

1935   Receives a BA in English and a diploma in education
        from Oxford.

1935–39 Golding says he "wasted" these four years as a so-
        cial worker in a London settlement house, at the
        same time writing, acting, and producing for a small
        "non-West-End" theater company.

1939   Marries Ann Brookfield, an analytical chemist, and
        begins teaching English and philosophy at Bishop
        Wordsworth's School in Salisbury, Wiltshire.

1940   With the outbreak of World War II Golding enlists
        in the Royal Navy where he spends the next five
        years.

1945   Returns to Bishop Wordsworth's school.

1954   *Lord of the Flies*, Golding's first published novel, is accepted by Faber and Faber after being rejected by twenty-one other publishers.

1955   *The Inheritors* is published. Golding becomes a fellow of the Royal Society of Literature.

1956   *Pincher Martin;* republished in the US as *The Two Lives of Christopher Martin* (1957).

1958   Golding's play, *The Brass Butterfly*, is performed at Oxford and then in London.

1959   *Free Fall* is published.

1960–62 Golding reviews books for the *Spectator*.

1960   April 20, *Miss Pulkinhorn*. BBC radio script.

1961   Completes his master of arts degree at Oxford and leaves teaching to devote full time to writing. March 19, *Break My Heart*, BBC radio script.

1961–62 Spends a year as writer in residence at Hollins College, Virginia, and on a lecture tour of other American colleges.

1964   *The Spire* is published.

1965   Golding is made a Commander of the British Empire (CBE).

1966   Golding's first book of essays, *The Hot Gates and Other Occasional Pieces*, is published; he becomes an honorary fellow of Brasenose College, Oxford.

1967   *The Pyramid* is published.

1970   Golding is awarded an honorary doctor of letters by Sussex University.

1971   *The Scorpion God: Three Short Novels* is published.

1979   *Darkness Visible* is published.

1980   *Rites of Passage* wins England's prestigious Booker McConnell Prize for the year's best novel.

1982   *A Moving Target*, a second book of Golding's essays, is published.

1983   Golding wins the Nobel Prize for Literature.

1984   *The Paper Men* is published.

1985   *An Egyptian Journal*, a record of Golding's travels in the country that preoccupied him from childhood, is published.

1987   *Close Quarters*, the second volume of a sea trilogy begun with *Rites of Passage*, is published.

1989   *Fire down Below* concludes the sea trilogy.

1

In Pursuit of Man:
The Dialectic of William Golding

"Put simply," said William Golding, accepting the 1983 Nobel Prize for Literature, "the novel stands between us and
the hardening concept of statistical man....It performs no
less an act than the rescue and the preservation of the individuality and dignity of the single being, be it man, woman
or child."[1] Implicit in this concept of the novel's humanizing
role is Golding's visceral distrust of the many formulae — invariably modern — that valorize the material at the expense
of the spiritual. Without subscribing to any single religion,
he is nonetheless an old-fashioned Christian moralist whose
novels characteristically depict the conflict between good and
evil within the human soul. In an age of unbelief founded on
technocratic rationalism Golding asserts the limits of human
knowledge and power. His is an eschatological fiction whose
characters are saved or damned according to their ability to
recognize and to overcome the darkness within. It follows
then that Golding's moral actors struggle not so much to
conquer the outer world as to master the inner self. Underlying his belief in man's essential depravity is a Calvinistic
sense of original sin. Nostalgia for an age of past innocence
as irrecoverable as it is remote intersects with the harrow-
ing awareness of present guilt. Although Golding traces his
own loss of innocence from World War II which exploded
his belief in "the perfectibility of social man" and convinced

him that man was "a morally diseased creature...a fallen being...gripped by original sin," his confidence in rationalism had long since been eroded.[2] Even as a child he had experienced "the looming terror which I knew night-long in my very bones." But his father's "exquisitely logical universe" from which God had been banished made no room for "the terrors of darkness."[3]

Born in Cornwall on September 19, 1911, William Gerald Golding belongs to that English generation whose parents were imbued with the nineteenth-century scientific rationalism of T. H. Huxley and H. G. Wells. Golding recalls the father who so profoundly influenced his early life as "incarnate omniscience. I have never met anybody who could do so much, was interested in so much, and who knew so much." To his son, Alec Golding bequeathed an interest in science and music as well as a "cosmology" flawed by its failure to accommodate "darkness and the irrational."[4]

When Golding went up to Brasenose College, Oxford, in 1930 to read science, he had yet to emerge from the long shadow of his father's influence. It was only because he thought that "it would hurt my father so much" that Golding delayed switching to English literature until his third year.[5] All along his first love had been poetry: "I have had a lifelong love of rhythm, sound, and in particular, rhyme."[6] From the age of seven, when he had "devoured" Tennyson, he had dreamed of writing poetry. At Oxford he produced in 1934 a slim volume that "ran to thirty-four pages and the verses ranged from four lines to twenty-eight" for Macmillan's *Contemporary Poets* series.[7] Virtually unnoticed when published and dismissed later by Golding as derivative juvenilia, the poems are chiefly noteworthy as symptoms of his growing disenchantment with rationalism. A typical poem, "Mr. Pope," satirizes the eighteenth-century apostle of rationalism who prefers the stars to "stand in rows all trim and neat." Another poem, "Vignette," skewers both the working-class rationalist who would storm the barricades and his conservative counterpart who

Puts back the ticking clock of heaven
And keeps the world at half-past seven.

After leaving Oxford in 1934 Golding was briefly involved with "a sort of fringe theatre...the Hampstead Everyman Theatre, Citizen House at Bath." Never more than "a hanger-on round the fringes" of the "professional stage scene," he "finally collapsed to the side, into teaching."[8] Still, the theater powerfully influences Golding's work, most obviously in *Pincher Martin* whose hero is a part-time actor, and in his one play, *The Brass Butterfly,* but also in the metaphorical texture of a novel such as *Rites of Passage.* After marrying Ann Brookfield in 1939, Golding settled into a position as schoolmaster at Bishop Wordsworth's School in Salisbury, where he remained with time off for wartime service in the Royal Navy (1940 to 1945) until 1961. Unlike his father, Golding was a reluctant schoolmaster: "I wasn't teaching because I wanted to teach, I was teaching because it was a way of earning enough money to keep myself alive while I moved towards other things."[9] Although he "found schoolmastering a chore," his years in the classroom contribute only less importantly than his experience of war to the making of *Lord of the Flies.* Golding's first published novel and still his most famous one, *Lord of the Flies* was hardly the overnight success of a youthful literary phenom. Already forty-three when he wrote the novel in an astoundingly brief three or four months, Golding had by then written several others that were rejected by publishers and subsequently discarded. Moreover, no fewer than twenty-one publishers rejected *Lord of the Flies* before Faber and Faber brought it out in 1954. Thereafter Golding's reputation grew steadily, as reflected in his election to the Royal Society of Literature (1955); his being made a CBE (1966); his winning of the Booker Prize, Great Britain's most prestigious literary award, for *Rites of Passage* (1980); and, of course, his loftiest honor, the Nobel Prize for Literature (1983).

Unlike most first novels, *Lord of the Flies* is the work of a fully mature writer. With each succeeding novel Golding does not so much develop new themes as play variations on the ones announced in *Lord of the Flies*. In "Fable," an essay largely concerned with intent and meaning in *Lord of the Flies*, Golding describes himself as a "fabulist" who, by "the nature of his craft...is didactic, desires to inculcate a moral lesson."[10] That lesson, foreshadowed by childhood terror of darkness and crystallized by World War II, is essentially antirationalistic. To a greater or lesser degree all of Golding's work follows *Lord of the Flies* in demarcating the limits of human reason. Man's endemic rage for order, incarnated in the clockwork theory of eighteenth-century rationalists, creates flawed or false models of the universe. For Golding, the universe is a "cosmic chaos" that resists simplistic patterning. A recurring character in his fiction is the one who, like Piggy in *Lord of the Flies*, tries futilely to impose an artificial order on "the natural chaos of existence." And the conventional image of human nature is no more reliable than the conventional belief in an ordered universe. Against fashionable behaviorist theories that externalize evil Golding opposes the distinctly unfashionable doctrine of original sin. Ralph's insight into the "darkness of man's heart" and his belated awareness of his own guilt (*Lord of the Flies*) is echoed in the experience of Jocelin (*The Spire*) and Colley (*Rites of Passage*). All three illustrate the persistent theme in Golding's work: "the fall from innocence or the loss of innocence."[11] Simon and Jack — saint and sinner — invoke the moral polarities of *Lord of the Flies*. Jack's conspicuous violations of the moral order for which Simon stands typify the workings of equally dark forces in Golding's ensuing fiction. Representatives of good and evil as starkly opposed as Simon and Jack consistently inhabit novels apparently designed to flesh out a Manichean worldview. But Golding's saintly exemplars of "the moral order as an attribute of the numinous" rarely survive.[12] After Simon, Nathaniel Walterson (*Pincher Martin*) and Matty Windrove (*Darkness Visible*) most obviously incarnate moral enlightenment. Their deaths, like Simon's, express the inhospitality of the modern world to its saints. Not surprisingly, their respective antitheses, Christopher Martin and Sophy Stanhope, are perhaps Golding's two most evil characters.

Although his themes and character types inevitably recur, Golding repeatedly invents new forms for his moral vision: "I would like my books to be as different from each other as possible, and so I don't notice the similarities."[13] Settings range from the prehistoric (*The Inheritors*, "Clonk, Clonk") to ancient Egypt ("The Scorpion God") to imperial Rome ("Envoy Extraordinary") to medieval England (*The Spire*) to the Napoleonic era (the sea trilogy) to modern times (*Lord of the Flies, Pincher Martin, Free Fall, The Pyramid, Darkness Visible, The Paper Men*). Whenever and wherever their location, the books display a dazzling array of narrative devices. Neanderthal perception shapes *The Inheritors; Pincher Martin* is enacted by its eponymous hero who apparently clings to a rock in mid-Atlantic but who is actually dead; *Free Fall* unfolds in a series of flashbacks; and the sea trilogy (*Rites of Passage, Close Quarters, Fire down Below*) revives the neoclassic epistolary novel in the form of Edmund Talbot's three journals. A complementary strategy is to invert or subvert the texts of other writers in order to invoke beliefs opposed to theirs. Thus *Lord of the Flies* adapts the mise-en-scène but refutes the childhood innocence of Ballantyne's *Coral Island;* and *The Inheritors* revises the brutish stereotype of Neanderthal man found in H. G. Wells's *Outline of History.* Variations on this tactic of creative usurpation account for the aura of prior texts in *Pincher Martin* (Defoe's *Robinson Crusoe*) and in *Free Fall* (Dante's *Divine Comedy*) as well as their specific evocation in the sea trilogy (Coleridge's "Rime of the Ancient Mariner").

If there is a writer whose books provide Golding with more than one-shot opportunities for textual revisionism, it is Joseph Conrad. More than any other single work, Conrad's *Heart of Darkness* seems to incarnate — most obviously in its title but also in its symbolism and morality — Gold-

ing's ethos. The progressive melting away of civilized values
in the forest (*Lord of the Flies*) and the civilized lies by
which Talbot determines to conceal the devastating truth
about Colley (*Rites of Passage*) particularly recall *Heart of
Darkness*. Traces of Herman Melville, whose *Billy Budd*
Golding forthrightly acknowledges to be the source of the
Billy Rogers character in *Rites of Passage,* are also apparent.
Like Melville, Golding evokes the primacy and universality
of evil, the alienation and guilt of man, the atavistic force
of the sea — all projections of two minds equally possessed
by the power of blackness. With Conrad and Melville Golding shares the fabulist's reliance on symbol and metaphor to
lend mythic resonance to his fables. Yet whatever his debt
to previous novels and novelists, Golding locates his literary models elsewhere: "I don't think my novels come out of
novels. If they owe anything to previous work ... it's the theatre." They have "a shape precisely like Greek drama ... this
rise of tension and then the sudden fall ... the character
who suffers a disastrous fall through a flaw in his character."[14] Although he refers to his "Aeschylean preoccupation
with the human tragedy," Golding implies that the theatricality of his work owes nearly as much to Shakespeare as
to the Greek tragedians: "I was more or less brought up
on Shakespeare and that has an influence ... I know my
Shakespeare pretty well by heart."[15] Perhaps the single most
striking example of theatricality occurs in *Pincher Martin*
where Aeschylean and Shakespearean drama converge in the
role-playing of its actor/hero. In the same novel, Golding's
third, the idea of theater as metaphor, appears for the first
time. *The Pyramid* and, especially, *Rites of Passage,* also rely
heavily on implicit or explicit evocations of the world as
theater.

   To encompass the world on a stage is to invoke the confined mise-en-scène of several Golding novels. The island of
Lord of the Flies, the rock of *Pincher Martin,* the cathedral
of *The Spire,* the ship of the sea trilogy — all are test-tube
environments that embody the radically limited conceptual

boundaries of their inhabitants. Settings and characteriza-
tions most often conspire to reveal the dark truths about
human nature. Man's inhumanity to man, rooted in original
sin and omnipresent in Golding's first three novels, continues unabated in his ensuing work. Beginning with *Free Fall,*
however, darkness becomes less the totality than a moiety
of the human condition. Redemption, conceivable in Sammy
Mountjoy's anguished self-analysis (*Free Fall*), is achievable
in Jocelin's deathbed revelation (*The Spire*). And Matty,
the unlikely Christ figure of *Darkness Visible,* becomes at
once the redeemer and the redeemed. In *Darkness Visible*'s
starkly opposed forces of light and darkness clashing on the
battlefield of a modern wasteland, Golding's profoundly religious vision achieves cosmic significance. His first work after
more than a decade of silence, *Darkness Visible* is also one
of his last to dramatize the eschatological implications of
human action.

Beginning with *Rites of Passage,* Golding's novels after
Darkness Visible are notably lighter in tone. Punctuated by
black comedy and even farce, they belie Golding's solemn reputation without subverting his moral intention. Like his earlier
works, they incarnate their author's rage to know "whatever
man is under the eye of heaven" in themes "of such a sort that
they might move us a little nearer that knowledge."[16] In his
long pursuit of what it is to be human Golding seems to have
modified his view that "history is really no more than a chronicle of original sin."[17] Calling himself "a universal pessimist
but a cosmic optimist," he envisions in man's conceptual limits — the very failures of perception that mark his characters'
moral blindness — the ironic key to redemption: "that the universe, the hell which we see for all its beauty, vastness, majesty
is only part of a whole which is quite unimaginable."[18] Whatever the composition of a cosmos whose ultimate reality must
forever elude us, its investigation remains central to the production of lasting art. Looking back on all of Golding's work,
James R. Baker thought that "in an atheistic age you have been
one who insists upon mystery, on the neglected or perhaps for-

gotten religious dimensions of human experience." Seconding
this view of his career as an essentially antimodern enterprise,
"a sort of counteraction," Golding not only revealed what he
set out to do but what he succeeded so powerfully in doing:
"I'd like to think it was a corrective to...a diminished sense
of the numinous."[19]

2

Grief, Grief, Grief:
Lord of the Flies

Lord of the Flies opens in Eden. Ralph, fair-haired protagonist, and Piggy, faithful companion and resident intellectual,
look about them and pronounce their island good. And so
it is, for William Golding has set his young castaways down
upon an uninhabited Pacific island as lush as it is remote. Fruit
hangs ripe for the picking; fresh water flows abundantly from
a convenient mountain; and the tropical climate soon prompts
the boys to throw off their clothes. Ralph joyfully stands on
his head, an action he will repeat at moments of high emotion.
It is easy to forget that the world is at war, and that the plane
that carried Ralph, Piggy, and the many other English boys
stranded on the island, was shot down by the enemy.
    As war and plane crash recede from memory, the visible
world shrinks to the desert island and its populace of six-
to twelve-year-old-boys. Because of the island's fecundity and
mild climate the boys are largely exempt from the struggle for
food and shelter; because of their youth they are exempt from
sexual longing and deprivation; because of their isolation they
are exempt from adult constraints. Free to live as they choose,
they can act out every boy's dream of romantic adventure until their eventual rescue. *Lord of the Flies* begins, therefore, as
a modern retelling of R. M. Ballantyne's Victorian children's
classic, *Coral Island*. Indeed Golding traces his book's genesis
to a night when he had finished reading just such an island
adventure story to his eldest child.[1] Exasperated by the famil-

iar cutout characters and smug optimism of the original, he conceived of breathing life into a moribund genre by isolating boys on a desert island and showing how they would *really* behave. Ballantyne's shipwrecked boys, somewhat older than Golding's, lead an idyllic life on their remote South Seas island. Tropical nature is benign, the boys' characters conventionally innocent. What evil exists on Coral Island enters in the form of such adult intruders as savage cannibals or pirates. Ballantyne's vision is doubly optimistic: man is inherently good; and good will win out in the end. Like most fairy tales, *Coral Island* is an amalgam of faith and hope.

On Golding's coral island, Piggy's allusions to atomic war, dead adults, and uncertainty of rescue barely ripple the surface of Ralph's pleasant daydreams. Soon the boys recover a conch from the lagoon. More than a plaything, the conch will become a means of communication, and ultimately a symbol of law and order. Instructed by the wise but ineffectual Piggy, Ralph blows on the conch, thereby summoning the scattered boys. Possession of the conch ensures Ralph's election as chief. Later the assembled boys agree that whoever wishes to speak must raise his hand and request the conch. Cradling the conch in one's hands not only confers instant personal authority but affirms the common desire for an orderly society.

Read as a social treatise, Golding's first chapter seems to posit notions of fair play and group solidarity familiar to readers of *Coral Island*. But the same chapter introduces us to Jack Merridew marching at the head of his uniformed column of choirboys. Clad in black and silver and led by an obviously authoritarian figure, the choirboys seem boy Nazis. Frustrated by Ralph's election as chief, Jack barely conceals his anger. The chapter ends with Jack, knife in hand, reflexively hesitating long enough on the downward stroke to allow a trapped piglet to escape. The civilized taboo against bloodletting remains shakily in place as the angry boy settles for slamming his knife into a tree trunk. "Next time," he cries.

It is the exploration of Jack's "next time" that will occupy much of the remainder of *Lord of the Flies*. By fixing incipient evil within Jack, Golding reverses the sanguine premise of nineteenth-century adventure stories that locate evil in the alien or mysterious forces of the outside world. According to Golding his generation's "liberal and naive belief in the perfectibility of man" was exploded by World War II. Hitler's gas chambers revealed man's inherent evil. His followers were not Ballantyne's savage cannibals or desperate pirates whose evil magically dissipated upon their conversion to Christianity. Rather they were products of that very Christian civilization that presumably guarantees their impossibility. Nor does it suffice to accept Ballantyne's implication that his boys' Englishness, like their Christianity, marks them as inevitably good. "We've got to have rules and obey them. After all, we're not savages. We're English, and the English are best at everything. So we've got to do the right things." Coming from Golding's Jack, these words effectively shatter Ballantyne's easy optimism. Conditioned no less by the theology of man's fall than by Nazi atrocities, *Lord of the Flies* traces the spreading stain of man's depravity from its first intimations in Jack to its near-total corruption of the boys and their social order. "I decided," explained Golding, "to take the literary convention of boys on an island, only make them real boys instead of paper cutouts with no life in them; and try to show how the shape of the society they evolved would be conditioned by their diseased, their fallen nature."[2]

Too immature to account for the enemy within, the boys project their irrational fears onto the outside world. The first of these projections takes the shape of a snakelike "beastie," the product of a small boy's nightmare. One side of the boy's face "was blotted out by a mulberry-colored birthmark," the visible sign of the dual nature of fallen man. More by force of personality than by reason, Ralph succeeds in exorcising the monster from the group consciousness. Now the boys struggle to drag logs up the mountain for a signal fire, Ralph and Jack bearing the heaviest log between them. Jack's momentary selflessness combined with the manipulation of the lenses of Piggy's spectacles to start their fire — as well as the very act of fire building itself — signal a resurgence of civilized values. But the fire soon rages out of control; exploding trees and rising creepers reinvoke cries of "Snakes!, Snakes"; and the small boy with the birthmark has mysteriously disappeared. The seed of fear has been planted. Reason has failed to explain the darkness within, and the island paradise begins its fatal transformation into hell.

Soon Ralph and Jack find communication impossible, the former talking of building shelters, the latter of killing pigs. Increasingly obsessed with his role as hunter, Jack neglects his more important role as keeper of the signal fire. Painting a fierce mask on his face he is "liberated from shame and self-consciousness." Shortly thereafter he and his frenzied followers march along swinging the gutted carcass of a pig from a stake to the incantory chant, "Kill the pig. Cut her throat. Spill her blood." Abandonment to blind ritual has displaced the reasoned discourse governed by the conch. Meanwhile the untended fire has gone out, and a ship has sailed past the island. Lost in blood lust, Jack's thoughts are far from rescue, and he at first barely comprehends Ralph's anger. When he does, he strikes out at the helpless Piggy, shattering one of his lenses. Reason henceforth is half-blind; the fragile link between Ralph and Jack snaps; and ritual singing and dancing resume as the boys gorge themselves on the slaughtered pig. That Ralph and Piggy join in the feast indicates the all-too-human failure to resist the blandishments of mass hysteria.

Killing marks the end of innocence. It is a wiser Ralph who "found himself understanding the wearisomeness of this life where every path was an improvisation and a considerable part of one's waking life was spent watching one's feet ... and remembering that first enthusiastic exploration as though it were part of a brighter childhood, he smiled jeeringly." Here at the beginning of the important fifth chapter, "Beast from Water," the regression and initiation themes converge. On the basis of his newfound knowledge, Ralph assembles the boys to discuss such practical matters as sanitation, shelter, and, most crucially, the keeping of the fire. But the tension among the boys is palpable, and Ralph soon confesses, "Things are breaking up. I don't understand why. We began well, we were happy." And he concludes, "Then people started getting frightened." Piggy's theory that life is scientific is countered by new reports of a beast from the sea. Neither Piggy's logic nor Ralph's rules can hold the boys together, and the meeting scatters in confusion.

E. M. Forster pleads in his introduction to the 1962 American edition of *Lord of the Flies* for more respect for Piggy.[3] Of course he is correct. Faced with specters of water beasts and Jack's authoritarian violence, who could fail to opt for Piggy's rationalism? Yet unaided reason cannot tell Ralph why things go wrong; it can only deny the physical reality of the beast. It is left to Simon, the skinny, inarticulate seer to "express mankind's essential illness" by fixing the beast's location: "What I mean is...maybe it's only us." Golding's moral — that defects in human society can be traced back to defects in human nature — can be illustrated by the fable of the scorpion and the frog:

> "Let me ride across the pond on your back," pleads the scorpion.
> "No," replies the frog, "for if I let you on my back your sting will prove fatal."
> "Listen to reason," cries the scorpion. "If I sting you, you'll sink to the bottom of the pond, and I'll drown."
> So the frog takes the scorpion on his back and begins swimming. Midway across the pond, he feels the scorpion's fatal sting. "How could you," gasps the frog with his dying breath. "Now you'll drown."
> "I couldn't help it," sighs the scorpion. "It's my nature."[4]

Though his irrationality, like the scorpion's, may cost him his life, man is his own worst enemy. Undone by the beast within, man self-destructs no matter what form of social organization he adopts.

"Beast from the Air" opens with the sign from the world of grown-ups that answers Ralph's desperate cry for help after the breakup of the assembly. Dropping from the air battle high above the island, a dead parachutist settles on the mountaintop where fitful breezes cause him spasmodically to rise and fall. This grotesque "message" recalls the adult savagery that marooned the boys on the island. Moreover, the boys now take the faraway figure for the beast that haunts their dreams. Confronted by its apparent physical reality even Ralph succumbs to fear. The ironic appropriateness of the man-beast foreshadows Jack's growing power and the final unraveling of the social order. Now that the primary task is to kill the beast, Jack assumes command. Promising hunting and feasting he lures more and more boys into his camp. Man regresses from settler to roving hunter, society from democracy to dictatorship.

It is at this point, shortly after the collapse of social order under the pressures of inherent evil associated with Jack and irrational fear embodied in the beast from the air, that Golding paints his most startling and powerful scene. Simon, the only boy who feels the need for solitude, returns to his place of contemplation, a leafy shelter concealed by the dense growth of the forest. There he witnesses the butchering of a frantically screaming sow, its gutting and dismemberment, and the erection of its bleeding head on a pole. This head, abandoned by the hunters as a "gift" to the beast, presides over a pile of guts that attracts great swarms of buzzing flies. And the Lord of the Flies speaks: "Fancy thinking the Beast was something you could hunt and kill. You knew didn't you? I'm part of you? Close, close, close! I'm the reason why it's no go? Why things are what they are?" Looking into the vast mouth, Simon sees only a spreading blackness into which he falls in a faint.

As previously noted, Golding has called himself a fabulist and his novel a fable. All fables contain morals; and the moral of *Lord of the Flies* is stated most explicitly in the confrontation between Simon and the pig's head. "I included a Christ-figure in my fable. This is the little boy Simon, solitary, stammering, a lover of mankind, a visionary."[5] Since the Lord of the Flies is Beelzebub, the Judeo-Christian prince of devils, the scene dramatizes the clash between principles of good and evil. To accept the consequences of Golding's symbolism is to recognize the inequality of the struggle between Simon and the head. The Lord of the Flies has invaded Simon's forest sanctuary to preach an age-old sermon: evil lies within man whose nature is inherently depraved. Simon cannot counter this lesson. Engulfed by the spreading blackness of the vast mouth, he is overwhelmed by Beelzebub's power and loses consciousness. While it does not necessarily follow that Christ's message is similarly overpowered by Satan's, the forest scene strongly implies that innocence and good intentions are lost amidst the general ubiquity of evil. That evil cannot be isolated in Jack or in the beast; it is "close, close, close," a part of all of us.

The Simon who awakens from his faint trudges out of the forest "like an old man," stooping under the heavy burden of revelation. Immediately he comes face-to-face with a second awful symbol of human corruption — the rotting body of the downed parachutist. It, too, has been found by the flies; like the pig's head it too has been reduced to a corrupt and hideous parody of life. Releasing the broken figure from the tangled parachute lines that bind it to the rocks, Simon staggers back down the mountain with his news that the beast is harmless. But he stumbles into the frenzied mob of dancing and chanting boys who take him for the beast, fall upon him, and tear him apart.

The ritual murder of Simon is as ironic as it is inevitable. Ironically, he is killed as the beast before he can explain that the beast does not exist. His horrid death refutes his aborted revelation: the beast exists, all right, not where we thought to find it, but within ourselves. Inevitably, we kill our savior who "would set us free from the repetitious nightmare of history."[6] Unable to perceive his truth, we huddle together in the circle of our fear and reenact his ritual murder, as ancient as human history itself. Golding's murderous boys, the products of centuries of Christianity and Western civilization, explode the hope of Christ's sacrifice by repeating the pattern of his crucifixion. Simon's fate underlines the most awful truths about human nature: its blindness, its irrationality, its blood lust.

That the human condition is hopeless is revealed in the fact that even Ralph and Piggy felt the need to join in the "demented but partly secure society" of the hunters just prior to Simon's murder. Later, they console themselves with the excuse that they remained outside the dancing circle. When Ralph recalls the horror of the murder, Piggy first tries to deny its reality. And when Ralph refuses to drop the subject, Piggy shrills again and again that Simon's death was an accident. His desperate rationalizations point to the inability of human reason to cope with the dark reality of human nature. Piggy's excuses are mere frantic attempts to explain away our basest instincts and actions. Their transparent failure to do so marks the limits of the human intellect. Symbolic of the fall of reason is the loss of Piggy's sight. His broken glasses, the means of fire making, are stolen in a raid by Jack and his hunters. As Jack stalks triumphantly off with the glasses dangling from his hand, the reign of savagery is all but sealed.

Jack's victory comes swiftly in the following chapter, "Castle Rock." Again Golding sets up a contest between principles of good and evil. But this time the outcome is a foregone conclusion. The pack of painted savages who blindly murdered Simon has by now abandoned all restraints. Personified by Roger, Jack's fanatical self-appointed "executioner," the hunters turn viciously against Ralph and Piggy and the twins Sam and Eric, the last four remnants of an orderly society. From high atop a cliff Roger pushes a great rock that, gathering momentum, strikes Piggy, killing the fat boy and shattering the conch. Although the conch has long since lost the power to invoke order, its explosion signals the final triumph of lawlessness. Screaming wildly, "I'm chief," Jack hurls his spear at Ralph, inflicting a flesh wound, and forcing the former chief to run frantically for his life.

"Cry of the Hunters," the novel's concluding chapter, marks the final degenerative stage in Golding's fable of man's fall. Ralph's pursuers, freed by Piggy's murder from the faint restraint of reason, have reduced Ralph to their quarry. As the savage pack closes in, the sad lesson of the hunt is inescapable:

not that the boys are dehumanized, but that they are all too human. Man's basic instinct is to kill; and the depth of his depravity is measured by the urge to kill his own species. Not only does the metaphor of the hunt complete Golding's definition of the human animal, but it forges a link to analogous hunts in Greek drama that loom in the background of *Lord of the Flies*.

Golding has often acknowledged the formative influence of the ancients. Together with the biblical version of man's fate expressed in the doctrine of original sin, Greek drama fleshes out the myth of the fall. If it is true that a writer's forebears surface most apparently in his early work, then the final hunt of *Lord of the Flies* is second only to Simon's "passion" in fixing the origins of Golding's most cherished ideas. While it is true that Simon's confrontation with the pig's head and his subsequent martyrdom are couched primarily in Christian terms, the Greek influence is also apparent. The pig's head is at once the Judeo-Christian Beelzebub and the king of the Olympian gods. Thus Jean-Paul Sartre's modern reworking of Greek motifs in *The Flies* opens on a public square in Argos, "dominated by a statue of Zeus, god of flies and death. The image has white eyes and blood-smeared cheeks."[7] Zeus himself appears in the play to explain the great swarms of buzzing flies that plague the city. "They are," he says, "a symbol," sent by the gods to "a dead-and-alive city, a carrion city" still festering fifteen years after the original sin of Agamemnon's murder. The citizens of Argos are "working out their atonement." Their "fear and guilty consciences have a good savor in the nostrils of the gods." Zeus implies that man's blood lust is balanced by his reverence for the gods, a view shared by Golding: "As far back as we can go in history we find that the two signs of man are a capacity to kill and a belief in God."[8] Human fear and guilt are perverse affirmations of the gods' existence and therefore find favor with the gods. For Sartre, the existential philosopher, man's awful freedom, won at the expense of breaking his shackles to the gods, is all-important. But for Golding, the Christian believer, man is lost without God. The absence of prayer, even among fearful young choirboys, is one of the darkest aspects of *Lord of the Flies*.

Although *The Flies* may have no direct bearing upon Golding's novel, its title as well as its identification of Zeus as god of flies and death reveal the same backdrop of Greek tradition. At the end of Sartre's play, the hero Orestes, drawn directly from Greek drama, is pursued by the shrieking Furies. No such deities hunt Ralph, only his fellow boys. Yet chase scenes of all kinds fill Greek drama, and Golding the classicist seems indebted not merely to the general metaphor of the hunt but specifically to its powerful treatment in two plays of Euripides: *The Bacchae* and *Iphigenia in Tauris*.

Euripides wrote *The Bacchae,* his greatest and most difficult play, in the wake of a disillusionment with the Peloponnesian War as profound as Golding's with World War II. As skeptical about human nature as Golding, Euripides had already written the most devastating antiwar play that survives from antiquity, *The Trojan Women*. Both *Lord of the Flies* and *The Bacchae* are anthropological passion plays in which individuals — children in Golding, adults in Euripides — revert to savagery and murder during a frenzied ritual.[9] At Thebes, where Dionysus (Bacchus) comes to introduce his worship to Greece, King Pentheus adamantly denies the new religion. To Dionysus's orgiastic revels Pentheus opposes the rule of reason. Yet he is tempted to disguise himself in the fawn skin of a Dionysian follower in order to watch the rites of the female devotees. Spied by the Bacchants, he is hunted down and torn to pieces by the frenzied women, led by his own mother, Agave. Maddened by the god, the hapless Agave bears Pentheus's head, which she imagines is a lion's, triumphantly back to Thebes. There she comes to her senses and awakens to the horrid proof of Dionysus's power. To deny Dionysus is to deny a fundamental force in human nature. That the destruction of Pentheus is so disproportionate to his offense constitutes poetic justice in *The Bacchae*: Pentheus denies the primitive power of unreason only to become its victim. Yet the orgiastic worship that transforms Agave into the unwitting murderess of her son is hardly preferable to Pentheus's denial. Euripides, in dramatizing the clash between emotionalism and rationalism, may be arguing the primacy of neither. However one interprets *The Bacchae,* its affinities with *Lord of the Flies* are striking:

Specifically, both drama and novel contain three interrelated ritual themes: the cult of a beast-god, a hunt as prefiguration of the death of the scapegoat-figure, and the dismemberment of the scapegoat. Golding deviates in only one respect from Euripides: logically Ralph, the Pentheus in embryo, should be the scapegoat; but the author assigns this role to Simon, allowing Ralph to live instead with his new-found knowledge of "the darkness of man's heart."[10]

Dionysus is the true hero of *The Bacchae;* his merciless destruction of Pentheus is but the opening salvo in his campaign to establish his worship in Hellas. Golding is no less concerned with the primitive force that Dionysus represents; but his primary concern is the impact of that force upon his hero. Ralph, the latter-day Pentheus, must therefore survive the ordeal of the hunt and live with his hard-won knowledge. Against the backdrop of the flaming island, a hell that once was Eden, the savage tribe pursues Ralph until, stumbling over a root, the frantic boy sprawls helplessly in the sand. Staggering to his feet, flinching at the anticipated last onslaught, Ralph looks up into the astonished face of a British naval officer. Ralph's miraculous salvation completes the drama of his initiation as, in a shattering epiphany, he weeps "for the end of innocence, the darkness of man's heart, and the fall through the air of the true wise friend called Piggy."

Although Golding shifts the focus from God's power to man's knowledge he relies on a familiar Euripidian device for ending his novel. Golding calls the timely arrival of the naval officer a "gimmick," a term subsequently used by critics to plague him. Yet the officer is neither more nor less than the Greek deus ex machina in modern uniform. Employed most strikingly by Euripides, the "god" in the machine is hoisted

high above the other actors to solve the problems of the preceding action and to supply a happy ending. Most often, when
the deity imposes a happy ending, the normal consequences
of the action would be disastrous. Neither *The Bacchae* nor
Sartre's *The Flies* employs the device in its purest form. In the
former, Dionysus resolves the action by heaping even more
woe upon the Thebans who denied his godhead. In the latter,
Sartre's Zeus absents himself from the ending, having already
explained its significance. Moreover, both gods take major
roles from the outset of their respective plays. Neither makes
the single in-the-nick-of-time appearance to reverse the action
that generally characterizes the deus ex machina.

In *Iphigenia in Tauris*, however, Euripides relies upon the
deus ex machina for a resolution markedly similar to that of
Lord of the Flies. Iphigenia, her brother Orestes, and his friend
Pylades, pursued by the minions of the barbarian king Thoas,
reach the seacoast where a Greek ship waits to carry them
home. But Thoas's troops control the strait through which
the ship must pass; and a strong gale drives the ship back toward the shore. Enter the goddess Athena, who warns Thoas
to cease his pursuit. It seems that the fates of Iphigenia and her
companions have been foreordained, and against this "necessity" even gods are powerless. Thoas wisely relents, the winds
grow favorable, and the ship sails off under Athena's divine
protection.

Barbarian pursuit, friendly ship, and miraculous rescue are
no less present in Golding's conclusion. And when to these
elements are added the hunt for sacrificial victims and the
bloody rites of the Taurian religion, the resemblances between
Iphigenia in Tauris and *Lord of the Flies* seem more than
skin deep. Yet the lessons of the two works radically differ.
Greek drama is ultimately conditioned by the proximity of
the gods: omnipresent yet inscrutable they influence human
action and determine human destiny. Since, as Sartre's Zeus
admits, the gods need mortals for their worship as much as
mortals need objects for their devotion, it follows that Greek
drama chronicles this interdependence. In *The Flies*, Sartre's

Zeus, the fading though still powerful king of the gods, owes his rule to human fear and superstition and relies upon man's willing servitude. When Orestes finally strides boldly into the sunlight, the spell of the gods is broken; henceforth he will blaze his own trail, acknowledging no law but his own. For Sartre, man's freedom begins with his denial of the gods and his full acceptance of responsibility for his actions and their consequences. And while existential freedom is as fearful as it is lonely, it is infinitely preferable to god-ridden bondage. Whether Dionysus stalking through *The Bacchae*, Athena watching over *Iphigenia in Tauris*, or Zeus brooding in *The Flies*, the gods play a role in the human drama. Note that all three deities carefully define their roles: Dionysus to punish the errant Thebans whose king denied him; Athena to ensure the proper worship of her sister, Artemis; and Zeus to warn the recalcitrant Orestes of the consequences of rebellion. So closely are the gods involved with mortals that their interventions, no matter how arbitrary, take on a certain inevitable logic.

What Golding calls the "gimmicked" ending of *Lord of the Flies* and the Greek deus ex machina used most conventionally in *Iphigenia in Tauris* are alike in their technical function: to reverse the course of impending disaster. Yet their effects are quite different. Athena's wisdom is incontrovertible, her morality unassailable. High above the awed mortals she dispels chaos and imposes ideal order. The very fact of her appearance underlines the role of the gods in shaping human destiny. Golding's spiffy naval officer is, however, no god. Nor does he represent a higher morality. Confronted by the ragtag melee, he can only wonder that English boys hadn't put up a better show, and mistakes their savage hunt for fun and games à la *Coral Island*. While he cannot know the events preceding his arrival, his comments betray the same ignorance of human nature that contributed to the boys' undoing. Commanding his cruiser, the officer will direct a maritime search-and-destroy mission identical to the island hunt. *Lord of the Flies* ends with the officer gazing at the cruiser, preparing to reenact the age-old saga of man's inhumanity to man.

Just as the naval officer cannot measure up to Euripides' Athena, so Ralph falls short of Sartre's Orestes. Orestes strides into the sunlight of his own morality to live Sartre's dictum that existence precedes essence. Creating himself anew with each action, he will become his own god. Ralph can only weep for the loss of innocence from the world; he shows no particular signs of coping with his newfound knowledge. To understand one's nature is not to alter it. Morally diseased, mired in original sin, fallen man can rise only by the apparently impossible means of transcending his very nature. In man's apparent inability to re-create himself lies the tragedy of *Lord of the Flies*. The futility of Simon's sacrificial death, the failure of adult morality, and the final absence of God create the spiritual vacuum of Golding's novel. For Sartre the denial of the gods is the necessary prelude to human freedom. But for Golding, God's absence leads only to despair and human freedom is but license. "The theme of *Lord of the Flies* is grief, sheer grief, grief, grief."[11]

3

Shadows of Forgotten Ancestors: *The Inheritors*

Lamenting anew the lost childhood of the world, William Golding turns from the remote island of *Lord of the Flies* to the remote time of *The Inheritors* (1955). The professional schoolmaster who sought the man in the boy now yields to the amateur archeologist who seeks the man in his ancestors:

For me, there is a glossy darkness under the turf, and against that background the people of the past play out their actions in technicolor. Sometimes I feel as though I have only to twitch aside the green coverlet of grass to find them there. Might I not come face to face with that most primitive of Europe's men — Neanderthal Man — who once loped along the track where I used to take my Sunday walk.[1]

The Inheritors is a fable of prehistory set at that precise moment when the last small band of Neanderthals is wiped out by advancing Homo sapiens.

Published only one year after *Lord of the Flies, The Inheritors* seems equally a product of wartime disillusionment. Again Golding overturns the comfortable assumptions of an earlier writer, in this case

the brash optimism that H. G. Wells exhibits in *The Outline of History*... Wells' *Outline of History* played a great part in my life because my father was a rationalist, and the *Outline* was something he took neat. Well now, Wells' *Outline of History* is the rationalist's gospel *in excelsis,* I should think. It seemed to me too neat and slick. And when I re-read it as an adult I came across his picture of Neanderthal man, our immediate predecessors, as being the gross brutal creatures who were possibly the basis of the mythological bad man, whatever he may be, the ogre. I thought to myself that this is just absurd. What we're doing is externalising our own inside.[2]

While this may be unfair to the Wells whose last book (*The Mind at the End of Its Tether,* 1946) recorded a postwar despair no less profound than Golding's, it accurately reflects the rationalist credo that Golding distrusts. As his epigraph to *The Inheritors* he quotes Wells's description of Neanderthal man in *The Outline of History:*

We know very little of the appearance of the Neanderthal man, but this . . . seems to suggest an extreme hairiness, an ugliness, or a repulsive strangeness in his appearance over and above his low forehead, his beetle brows, his ape neck, and his inferior stature. . . . Says Sir Harry Johnston, in a survey of the rise of modern man in his *Views and Reviews:* "The dim racial remembrance of such gorilla-like monsters, with cunning brains, shambling gait, hairy bodies, strong teeth, and possibly cannibalistic tendencies, may be the germ of the ogre in folklore."

Golding's Neanderthals resemble Wells's only in outward appearance. Far from the ogres of folklore, they are innocents whose ignorance of violence and evil makes them easy prey for ruthless Homo sapiens. Like the various "beasts" of *Lord of the Flies,* the Neanderthals are convenient projections of the darkness within man.

A good part of *The Inheritors* is devoted to painting a composite picture of Neanderthal life. Lok, the young male through whose sensory perceptions most of the action is filtered, is one of eight surviving members of his tribe. The little band is led by the aged and ailing patriarch, Mal, whose apparent wife — referred to simply as the "old woman" — is later revealed to be Lok's mother. Ha, the third male, mates with Fa, as does Lok: Neanderthal sexuality is polygamous though not promiscuous. Nil carries her baby, the "new one," and Liku, a young girl, bears the "little Oa," a doll representing the tribe's mother goddess. "A woman for Oa and a man for the pictures in his head," runs Neanderthal wisdom, alluding not only to the most important functions of the two sexes but also to their interdependence. As Oa's priestess, the old woman is the locus of religious belief and custom, the guardian of fire and of the life force itself. Mal's leadership is expressed through "pictures" — the mostly intuitive Neanderthal approximation of thought — which he communicates to his followers. Even when the accuracy of Mal's pictures is suspect — as when he leads the people's annual springtime migration too early — momentary trepidation dissolves into instinctive obedience. For Mal's is the voice of tradition as well as the voice of wisdom and experience, and the same intuition that looks to the old woman for values looks to Mal for guidance.

Sharing pictures, like sharing food or fire or water, is symptomatic of the intensely communal Neanderthal way of life. Often cold and hungry, the people huddle together around the fire, consoled by Mal's tales of former leaders harking back to an Edenic past. Once there had been many people and a land of perennial summer where "flowers and fruit hung on the same branch." Life began with Mother Oa, who "brought forth the earth from her belly. She gave suck. The earth brought forth women and the first man out of her belly." In the Neanderthal scheme of things the creative force is vested not in God the Father but in God the Mother. Their matriarchal religion incarnates this principle of female creativity in the goddess Oa; to her the people owe not only their genesis but the life-sustaining abundance that she brings forth from the earth. Despite the great fire that reduced them to their present number, the people continue to respect all natural occurrences as evidence of Oa's creative handiwork. And their animism extends to a reverence for all life and a consequent horror of bloodletting. Among the people violence and murder are unknown, and weapons do not exist. Killing, even for food, is forbidden, although carrion and the leavings of predators may be eaten. Still, when Lok and Fa tear apart and eat the body of a doe recently killed by a "cat," they feel guilty. The air around the doe seems "forbidding with violence and sweat, with the rich smell of meat and wickedness." A creature of Oa's, the doe retains a certain sanctity even in death.

The lingering dread inspired by eating even a slain doe reflects the people's belief in the sacredness of all life, a likely by-product of their matriarchal religion. Sitting before their fire sharing doe meat, the people imagine the doe's "strength and fleetness" flowing into the dying Mal when he eats of the "soft brain." The sense of a bond among all living things is most evident, however, in the collective life of the people. So intense is their communal sympathy that the others shiver when Mal shivers, laugh when Lok laughs. The extended family that comprises the people is itself the product of a communal value system. Although each one of them plays a separate and clearly defined role in the collective life of the group, personal identity is less an individual than a tribal attribute. No one man or woman has proprietary claims on another: Lok and Ha share sex with Fa and Nil as instinctively as they share food and fire. And all press close to the dying Mal, trying to warm his body with theirs. The patriarch's death creates a "blankness" in their midst that saps their collective strength.

"Oa has taken Mal into her belly," explains the old woman. Implicit in her trope of birth reversed is the people's acceptance of death as a natural and inevitable part of life. In their matriarchal worldview, birth and death are complementary episodes in the unending drama of feminine creation. From Oa comes everything — the abundance of nature, the life-sustaining though fearsome fire — necessary for survival. And although Oa's world is not static — seasons pass, people age and die — it is in its apparent predictability essentially unchanging. So long as nature conforms to their conviction that "today is like yesterday and tomorrow," their uncritical acceptance of what life brings is as harmonious as it is naive. Satiated with doe meat, the people feel that "Life was fulfilled,

there was no need to look further for food, tomorrow was secure and the day after that so remote that no one would bother
to think of it." At such times — and others when they are clus-
tered together in the overhang around the fire — their sense
of well-being is characteristically expressed in a "timeless silence." The Neanderthal language is fit primarily to ratify
experience in memory rather than to transmit ideas. Once
sealed in the collective consciousness, images of the world
can be called up in the form of "pictures." Via the formula
"I have a picture," the people evoke memories of communal
experiences as modes of communication. In the absence of
precedent, the people can summon few "pictures"; they are
tongue-tied in the presence of the new.

Reflected in the unevolved language of the Neanderthals is
their inability to adapt to changing conditions. When today
turns out not to be like yesterday, they are powerless to effect
their fate. While they are inevitably victimized by the far more
intelligent Homo sapiens, the newcomers merely apply the
coup de grace to a foredoomed people. Even before the coming
of the new men, the year-round summer when "flowers and
fruit hung on the same branch" is no more. The passing of that
idyllic world is finalized by the death of old Mal, the last of the
people who can recall their lost paradise. And the premature
return of the people to their summer habitat presages not only
Mal's decline but the loss of Eden. His apocalyptic vision of
the burning forest signals the catastrophic transformation of
the Neanderthal world and the impending annihilation of the
Neanderthals themselves. Food is scarcer: the people search
in vain for the once-plentiful berries and honey. That any
change, no matter how insignificant, is fraught with danger for
the innocent people is apparent in the initially comic episode
of the missing log. The log's disappearance prefigures that
of the Neanderthal species, commencing with the death of
Mal, the patriarch and indispensable leader. Fa's conclusion
that "the log that was not there" killed him is literally true
in the sense that Mal was done in by change, the force that
will undo them all.

With the death of Mal and the disappearance of Ha, the tight social fabric binding the people together begins to unravel. Even before Mal dies, Lok senses the altered geometry of their existence. Although he has yet to sight one of the new men, the scent and sound of the "other" have "tugged at the strings" that bind Lok to his own kind. Instinctively he senses the threat to Neanderthal survival implicit in the loosening of the ties that bind: "The strings were not the ornament of life but its substance. If they broke a man would die." Lok's fears prefigure his own eventual isolation and death. Directly attributable to the presence and pressure of Homo sapiens, the extinction of Lok and his tribe is inevitable in any case. Theirs is the fate shared by all unadaptable species. The new men — the inheritors — possess the requisite intelligence for survival that their victims so notably lacked. With intelligence, however, comes the aggressiveness and cruelty that were just as conspicuously absent from the Neanderthals' makeup. *The Inheritors* — like *Lord of the Flies* — makes it clear that the meek shall not inherit the earth while at the same time looking askance at those who do.

The ugly traits that ensure the survival of the new people and hasten the destruction of the old are documented in the successive fates of the Neanderthals. One by one they are killed off by the "other" whose murderous instincts seem second nature. The poisoned arrow shot at Lok epitomizes the actions of the new people. All that remains of the missing Ha is "a dirty smudge on the earth where the fire had been." Presumably he has been killed and eaten, a fate that later befalls Liku. The murder of Nil and the old woman and the seizure of the new one, all of whom pose no threat to their assailants, further demonstrates the inherently violent disposition of the new men. It is the cannibalization of Liku, however, that most dramatically spotlights the differences between Homo neanderthalis and Homo sapiens. The relish with which the new people consume flesh powerfully contrasts with the trepidation felt by the Neanderthals when they ate the doe. That the inheritors hold life cheaper than did the Neanderthals is but one of Golding's many ironies. Reverence for life becomes anachronistic, an attribute to be cast off as incompatible with human development, an impediment to evolutionary progress. Clearly superior to Homo neanderthalis on a rational level, Homo sapiens is vastly inferior to him on a moral level.

The many moral and intellectual contrasts between the "people" and human beings are detailed in the second half of *The Inheritors*. Everything about the humans — their appearance, their behavior, their religion — is diametrically opposed to the Neanderthals. Less robust, more easily tired, Homo sapiens is physically inferior. While the Neanderthals' matriarchal religion emphasized the separate functions of the sexes, it valued men and women equally. Under the patriarchal system of the humans, however, women are regarded as inferior to men. As mere chattels to be possessed, human women exacerbate the already aggressive rivalries of their men. Thus Marlan, the witch doctor/priest of the stag religion, has stolen the voluptuous Vivani from her husband; he and his small band of followers are renegades fleeing the wrath of their tribe. Tuami also wants Vivani; the ivory knife he fashions may one day be used on Marlan. Religious observance is shot through with the same violence that underlies sexual relations. The worship of the stag is reminiscent of the boys' obeisance before the boar's head in *Lord of the Flies*. And the sacrifice and cannibalization of Liku is only an extreme instance of the predatory religious frenzy that made a sacrificial victim of Simon. This human penchant for victimizing one's own species characterizes the rites of the stag religion. Although the new men refrain from cannibalizing their own (Liku is not "human") they mime human sacrifice in rituals of mutilation: Pine-tree's finger is cut off as an offering to the stag-god.

In addition to this mutilation, Lok and Fa witness the lust, drunkenness, and selfishness that also characterize human behavior. Like Adam and Eve after eating of the apple, the last Neanderthals are forced to partake of the knowledge of evil. The Eden myth is further invoked in the tree from which they spy unseen on the new people. By climbing Golding's tree of knowledge, however, Lok and Fa follow an upward rather than a downward path to wisdom. In this apparent reversal of the Judeo-Christian scenario, the tree becomes an ambivalent symbol of the symbiotic relationship between evolutionary rise and moral decline. What Lok and Fa witness from the tree is nothing less than a psychodrama in which as spectators they vicariously participate. Prelapsarian innocents, they encounter for the first time the dark mysteries of human nature and are propelled into the postlapsarian world. Their fall into knowledge takes the form of emulating human behavior. After downing the heady alcoholic brew — Golding's version of the forbidden fruit of Genesis — left behind by the humans, Lok drunkenly declares: "I am one of the new people." Newly initiate, he has begun the arduous process of separating himself from the exterior world, of straining toward the self-consciousness that defines individual identity.

Lok's heightened perception is flickering rather than steady. Even before he achieves via alcohol his closest proximity to the human condition, he had moments when "it seemed to him that his head was new." In a momentary flash of insight he intuits the murderous designs of the new men "who would kill him if they could" and simultaneously guesses Ha's fate. As he strains to see more pictures, however, his head empties, and he is again only Lok. Still, he has acquired, along with fear of the new men and a consequent sense of his own imperiled existence, the habit of thought: "Lok discovered 'like.' " Although he can exercise his newfound reasoning ability only sporadically, it enables him to comprehend the new men who are "like wolves" but who are also "like Oa." Lok's similes alter his relationship to the external world. To perceive by analogy is to abandon an intuitive understanding of the world for a conceptual one. Eddying helplessly between divergent worldviews, Lok becomes intellectually more than Neanderthal while remaining intellectually less than human. With the gradual emergence of self-consciousness, Lok can no longer enjoy the "mindless peace" of the Neanderthals. He suffers a loss of innocence that takes the form of a terrifying disjunction between the inner and outer Lok. At the same time, "the convulsion of the understanding" that he has experienced falls short of the full self-consciousness of Homo sapiens.

Lok's stumbling emergence from undifferentiated consciousness to the brink of conscious individuality underscores the differences between the Neanderthals and their successors. No longer at home in the universe, the new people "are frightened by the air." In their fragmented world, chaos is the rule, harmony the exception. Because of the inward terror of an existence defined essentially by alienation from nature and from one another, Homo sapiens is a predator. The ritual sacrifice and eating of Liku ("like you"?) dramatizes the human rapaciousness that all too commonly takes the form of scapegoating and bloodletting. Not only is worship equated with sacrifice, so is eating with cannibalism. Sexual relations, for example, are equally predatory. Proprietary and exploitive, they mirror the same patterns of aggression and domination that characterize nearly every aspect of human behavior. As Lok grows more and more aware of the dichotomy between man and outer reality, he increasingly falls prey to the same anxieties that bedevil the new men. The use of likeness as a tool of perception reflects his loss of oneness (Oaness?) with nature. In the similes that express likeness lies the recognition of a dissociated universe that can no longer be explained by spontaneous "pictures." Pictures once sufficed to evoke the simple certainties of life as it was; they are pathetically inadequate to cope with the complex contingencies of life as it has become. Yet the habit of thought demanded by a dissociated universe can never be more than a sometime thing for Lok. Too low on the evolutionary ladder ever to acquire the requisite mental agility, Lok and his kind are foredoomed to extinction.

Their eventual annihilation is implicit in the structure of *The Inheritors*. With each succeeding chapter the Neanderthal band grows smaller. As its numbers dwindle, the pace of the novel quickens as if to signal that time is rapidly running out for the few remaining Neanderthals. For Lok and Fa, the last Neanderthal adults, the fear of extinction grows palpable, especially given the probability that Fa is barren. Desperation and wishful thinking intersect in her pathetic assurance to Lok: "There will be a fire again. And I shall have children." Even more pathetic is Lok's attempt to rescue the already cannibalized Liku. Rightly intuiting that hope for Neanderthal survival must not depend upon Fa's questionable fertility but ignorant of Liku's fate, Lok wastes the chance to snatch the new one (the only real, albeit slim hope for a Neanderthal future) in futile search for Liku. Owing to the intensely communal nature of Neanderthal life, their successive losses sharply affect the survivors. When the temporarily separated Lok and Fa are reunited, they cling tightly to each other, repeating "It is bad to be alone." After the wounded Fa is swept over the waterfall to her death and Lok is left alone, his own imminent death is a foregone conclusion. That the lone individual cannot survive is axiomatic for the Neanderthals.

What Lok most fears — aloneness — epitomizes the human condition. Alienation — from nature and from one another — spawns the fear and aggression that seem endemic in the new people. Unlike the gentle Neanderthals whose religion forbids even the killing of animals, Homo sapiens thrives on violence. The new men are hunters and flesh-eaters with teeth like the fangs of wolves. Even their lovemaking is a "wolf-like battle" devoid of tenderness. As witnessed by Lok and Fa, sex between Tuami and Vivani is mutually voracious. Bloody and brutal, the lovemaking episode reflects the general belligerence of personal relationships based not upon communion but consumption. The cannibalization of Liku is merely the most horrendous example of the new people's urge to consume. They respond to the unknown not with the innocent curiosity of the Neanderthals but with an instinctive reflex to attack. At first sight of Lok, a new man instantly fires a poisoned arrow at the bemused Neanderthal who, ignorant of the concept of weaponry, takes it for a twig. Later in the novel, Lok, by now fully aware that the new men are out to kill him, still remains incapable of matching their aggressiveness, even in self-defense. Unlike Homo sapiens, who lashes out at all threats — real or imagined — the placid Neanderthal can respond to threats only by flight and finally, alone and distraught, by curling into the fetal position in preparation for death.

The aggressiveness of the new people is clearly associated with their individualism — just as nonviolence is associated with the communal Neanderthals. Because each new man is finally alone with himself, he is bereft of the fellowship that assuages fear. While the Neanderthals learn to fear (justifiably) the "other," they are at ease among themselves and in nature. The "advanced" society of Homo sapiens is fueled by the will to dominate rather than to cooperate; and the common good takes a backseat to individual gain. Although their minds are far more highly developed than those of the Neanderthals, the new men are naturally distrustful and wary of their fellows, whom they rightly regard not as allies but as competitors. Just as their blunted senses have alienated them from nature, so their calculating minds alienate them from each other. And it is their alienation and self-consciousness that may chiefly account for their violence — in lovemaking, in worship, even in cannibalism. At the same time, however, episodes of violence may be interpreted not only as typical acts of asserting but also as desperate attempts at escaping the human condition. That condition, rooted in loneliness, is, of course, inescapable. In his furtive lovemaking and excessive drinking, early Homo sapiens previews the modes of escape — equally futile — that will occur to his successors. One of the most striking of the many ironies of *The Inheritors* is that in getting drunk Lok comes closest to being human.

That Lok can never become fully human is his tragedy — and his triumph. Unintelligent but amply endowed with the virtues of warmth, empathy, and compassion, Lok may be too "human" — in the highest sense of the term — for his own good. What he lacks is the capacity for selfishness, brutality, and betrayal — those attributes of the intelligence that

ensure survival. Never can Lok and his kind bridge either
of the two falls that separate them from the inheritors. Just
as the waterfall marks the edge of geographical possibility
for the Neanderthals, so the biblical fall marks the limit of
their knowledge. Water, merely navigable for Homo sapiens,
proves disastrous for Neanderthals (Mal, Fa). Similarly, the
postlapsarian humans can navigate the sea of knowledge in
ways undreamed of by their prelapsarian predecessors. The
Neanderthals of *The Inheritors* can only react to nature, never
master it. They are gatherers, at the mercy of nature's bounty;
the new people are hunters, ripping what they need from nature. Controlled by a chancy environment — unseasonable
cold, a missing log — the Neanderthals exist in evolutionary gridlock. Homo sapiens is alone capable of evolutionary
progress. Possessed of postlapsarian intelligence and its ac-
companying ruthlessness, the new men are able not only to
fashion boats for locomotion but weapons for killing. Their
advanced technology converts the fearsome barrier the river
presented to the Neanderthals into a harmless waterway as
easily as it converts the innocent creatures of nature into food.

Among the creatures of nature that must inevitably fall prey
to man is Lok whose position on the evolutionary ladder is
clarified once and for all midway through chapter 11. Of the
twelve chapters of *The Inheritors,* the first eleven chronicle
the gradual destruction of the Neanderthals from their own
perspective. As their band dwindles, the field of vision corre-
spondingly narrows. Finally there remains only Lok, the first
Neanderthal to appear in the novel and the last to leave it. It
is immediately after Fa has dropped over the waterfall to her
death and Lok is left alone that the Neanderthal point of view
is abandoned. Essentially communal, Neanderthal perception
is effectively snuffed out at that moment (i.e., the death of
Fa) when a community no longer exists. What humanity the
Neanderthals possessed was conferred by communal bonding; alone, Lok is reduced to his individual (i.e., subhuman)
genetic coding. His diminished status is reflected in a startling
shift of narrative perspective: the suddenly dehumanized Lok

is no longer "he" but "it" — a "red creature." Although the creature running is reminiscent of an earlier Lok who ran "as fast as he could" in the first sentence of *The Inheritors,* it is merely a strange hairy beast as seen from the newly objective angle of vision. This narrative distancing is signaled on the page by the wider spacing that separates the two versions of Lok. The remainder of chapter 11 follows the red creature to its death and functions as a kind of coda, bridging the evolutionary gap between the Neanderthal perspective of the first eleven chapters and the human perspective of the twelfth.

Tuami, the central consciousness of the new people, occupies the foreground of chapter 12. His narrative displacement of Lok, equivalent to the evolutionary displacement of Neanderthal by Homo sapiens, is accompanied by a mode of perception far in advance of simple "pictures." By radically foreshortening evolutionary time — the brief chapter 11 coda seems to bridge eons as well as species — Golding accentuates the intellectual superiority of the inheritors. At the same time, however, he reiterates what the preceding action illustrates: that each rung of the evolutionary ladder is won at great cost. Human consciousness is indisputably a great asset; but its price is the knowledge of, and inevitably the practice of, evil. Tuami busily sharpens a knife to be used against Marlan, the priest/leader of their band and his rival for Vivani, the femme fatale whose allure drove Marlan to kidnap her from her husband. Vivani embodies in a sexual context the same discordance in the human condition evidenced by Tuami's knife sharpening. The knife itself, like the arrows shot at the Neanderthals, epitomizes the aggressive nature of the new men. Fear both triggers and exacerbates their aggressiveness. Projected onto the innocent and harmless Neanderthals, fear, ever present among the new people, conditions their dealings with others no less than their attitudes toward the outside world. Already dramatized in totemic and sacrificial worship, their fear of one another is likewise manifest in a hierarchical social structure whose nature is most fully revealed in chapter 12 when Twall and Vakiti call Tuami "master." In the dugout Vakiti steps gingerly around Marlan, giving him as wide a berth as possible. This instance of the typical pattern of dominance and subjection that shapes human society begs the contrast with the closeness of Neanderthal interpersonal relationships. Humans keep away from one another; the people clung together.

Just as Neanderthal interdependence was embodied in Lok, so human isolation is represented by Tuami who is always "standing to one side as though he were of a different people." Even in a society in which the rule of every man for himself seems to govern human intercourse, Tuami's is an extreme form of estrangement. Always the observer, rarely the participant, he professes the aloof detachment of the artist, a recurring figure in Golding's fiction: "In fact, there is a good deal about the artist in all my books... Tuami, yes, he has the instincts from the start."[3] Tuami's artistic "instincts" become conduits of moral revelation. More sensitive than the others, he is most aware of his guilt. And with the dawn of self-understanding comes a sensation of powerlessness against a "world of confusion." No longer does he care about finishing, his mind now converts the blade of his dagger from an instrument of murder into a token of futility: "What was the use of sharpening it against a man? Who would sharpen a point against the darkness of the world?" Thus far, Tuami's growth is expressed as a negative capability but an important one nonetheless. By dropping his plot against Marlan, Tuami — uncharacteristically for Homo sapiens — has recognized the limits of violence. Golding expresses Tuami's ultimate insight by further refining the symbolism of the knife. Drawn by his raised consciousness away from the knife's murderous potential and toward a perception of its powerlessness to dispel the world's darkness, Tuami is momentarily "tempted to throw the thing overboard." What distracts him is the mother/child tableau presented by Vivani and the "devil" (the "new one" captured from the Neanderthals) entwined. It is their shape that Tuami begins to "feel" in his hands and that lies "waiting in the rough ivory of the knife-haft that was so much more important than the blade." The knife has undergone its final symbolic metamorphosis from a tool of murder into the stuff of art, from a reminder of death to a promise of life. Further, by locating Tuami's inspiration in the mother and child, Golding invokes what is arguably the single most important pictorial subject in Western (i.e., Christian) art. As such, it expands Tuami's as yet unrealized ivory sculpture into a symbol not merely of personal but of universal redemption. Even in its simplest application, shorn of its religious implications, the conversion of the knife from an instrument of destruction into a means of creation signals the human capacity for good as well as evil.

Implicit in the knife's dualism is man's double nature. The blade of evil is as much a part of the knife as the ivory haft of good. Marlan persistently — and mistakenly — externalizes human evil, projecting the darkness within onto the "devils" without. To escape the darkness it is necessary only to "keep to the water," safe from the "forest devils" who "cannot pass over water." Tuami knows better. Echoing Marlan, he calls the Neanderthals devils, but Tuami also discovers the personal demons that cannot be exorcised merely by assigning them to a convenient scapegoat. What makes Tuami fully human — and distinguishes him from Marlan and the others — is not only his awareness of the guilt that all men share but his capacity for shaping it into a creative force. Thus the "red devil" is imaginatively transformed into the holy infant of Christian iconography. That the humans take a Neanderthal child with them is itself significant. Because Tuami's vision of the mother-and-child cannot but invoke Jesus, the baby becomes the little child that will lead them. For, according to Golding, "the new people haven't got an Oa. They haven't got a concept of the universal God yet. That's what they're going to get and they'll get it maybe partly through the new one, the little red devil."[4] In Golding's moral calculus, "the good qualities of the Neanderthal people" are crucial to the "emergent humanity" of Homo sapiens. Again the captive baby, in whom Neanderthal goodness is incarnated and through whom it may be transmitted to the inheritors, is of vital importance. The baby will grow up "to be at once a source of fear and love among the new people," a "shaman" whose "powers... they will regard as unnatural, superhuman."[5] To be fully human the new people must overcome their fear of the "red devil" in their midst and, through love of him, achieve the "concept of the universal God."

It is Golding himself who suggests this optimistic scenario but only by way of arguing that *The Inheritors,* like any complex work of art, "must be susceptible to multiple interpretations." The hope — embodied in the Neanderthal baby — for a fundamental change in human consciousness exists only as potential. Tuami's successive epiphanies involving the metamorphosis of the knife from malevolent instrument into beneficent artifact arguably constitutes proof positive of his "emergent humanity." Yet there is no evidence that his companions share his insight. As artist and seer Tuami represents not ordinary but exceptional man. The possibility that he can effect the necessary change in the hearts and minds of his contemporaries may prove as remote for Tuami as it will for his successors in millennia to come. *The Inheritors* ends with Tuami straining to make out "what lay at the other end of the lake" but unable to "see if the line of darkness had an ending." This prospect of unending darkness recalls the conclusion of *Lord of the Flies* where it also serves as a metaphor for the human condition. Although light (symbol of Tuami's artistic insight) flashes briefly on the waters, it is into the gathering darkness that the new people sail. As in *Lord of the Flies,* darkness shrouds the action of *The Inheritors,* much of which takes place at night. Twilight, shadow, sunset, and finally the extinguished fire presage the end of Neanderthal life. Lok, reduced to a shadow, his red body turned gray and blue in the twilight, curls into a fetal position to die. Earlier, darkness had characterized a Neanderthal mind empty of pictures, just as it later characterizes a human mind filled with evil intent. Golding's point is that both races walk in darkness, a darkness perhaps even more profound for the inheritors than it was for their victims.

Golding has long maintained that, of all the novels he has written, *The Inheritors* is his favorite. Like the archeology to which he is so strongly attracted, the Neanderthals of *The Inheritors* incarnate the "days of innocence" and provide a way of escape from a world of sin. Among Golding's novels only *The Inheritors* is set in a past so remote as still to be pristine. "As long as you have had Homo sapiens, you have had wickedness," claims Golding, "because that's what he's about."[6] No matter that the new people are ourselves and that we in them are the beneficiaries of an evolutionary process as inexorable as it is cruel. What happens in *The Inheritors* conforms to Golding's views of evolution: "I picture the Neanderthals as a primitive but good race that existed before the Fall, wiped out by Homo sapiens simply because it wasn't evil enough to survive."[7] It is true that Tuami's belated self-awareness evokes a measure of sympathy for fallen man, sentenced to navigate perilous waters amidst gathering darkness. Yet the preceding eleven chapters have effectively demolished the Wellsian view that Homo sapiens is in every respect the superior of Homo neanderthalis. Although the fall from, or loss of, innocence is Golding's persistent theme, never does he equate evolution with progress. The human world of masters and slaves, victimizers and victims can hardly be considered an improvement on the Neanderthal world of communal egalitarianism. Again and again Golding subverts the received evolutionary wisdom. Lok is reduced to a creature not primarily by the impersonal forces of evolution but by the personal evil of the new men. Even as a creature he cries for his lost companions and dies of heartbreak at being left alone. In Lok's tears, as in the many prior instances of Neanderthal bonding, Golding evokes a deeper "humanity" than the humans possess. Tuami, in the rush of guilt that accompanies self-awareness, cries out: "What else could we have done?" Anguished by his role in wiping out the Neanderthals, Tuami never doubts its necessity. Reason, man's highest faculty, can do no better than valorize murder as the necessary response to the outside world. *The Inheritors* follows *Lord of the Flies* in depicting evil not as aberrant but as inherent in human nature.

In "Digging for Pictures," Golding recalls a "time when excavation left me with something like a load of guilt." Still a boy, the future author encounters for the first time the bits and pieces of a vanished world that his mature imagination will one day reanimate in *The Inheritors*. The pictures of the essay's title and "the piece of chalk which might have been the head of a doll" (i.e., the little Oa) respectively evoke the Neanderthal mind and religion. Unearthing a pile of bones, the young Golding imagines them belonging to a "family from the days of innocence" who "could not match our wickedness." Although he perceives the folly of identifying himself "with people without first knowing what sort of people they are," he instinctively does so anyway. Welded to them by his imagination, he acknowledges his share in their "prehistoric murder." "Digging for Pictures" records the loss of innocence triggered by consciousness of the universal guilt of postlapsarian man. That guilt, extending back to Tuami and forward into the indefinite future and consequent upon the darkness within Homo sapiens — the inherent evil that no degree of further evolution may eradicate — was nonexistent in Homo neanderthalis. Only by calling up the shadows of forgotten ancestors — our murdered better selves — may Homo sapiens even begin to approximate Homo moralis.

4

A Double Dying: *Pincher Martin*

Man's predatory nature — as salient in the modern youths of *Lord of the Flies* as it was in their ancient forebears in *The Inheritors* — is incarnated in the eponymous hero of *Pincher Martin* (1956). Human history, for Golding, is a chronicle of the original sin that shapes and motivates us: "Our nature is to want to grab something that belongs to somebody else, and we have either to be taught or teach ourselves that you've got to share, you can't grab the lot."[1] Nicknamed Pincher, as are all Martins in the Royal Navy, Golding's embodiment of greed has uncompromisingly and unceasingly striven to "grab the lot" — to pinch is to steal. It is, however, the very enormity of his greed that, despite his common surname, denies Martin archetypal status. Golding, ever the moralist, invokes the wages of sin, sounding his cautionary note by exaggerating in Martin the nature common to us all: "He's fallen more than most. In fact I went out of my way to damn Pincher as much as I could by making him the nastiest type I could think of."[2] Although *Pincher Martin* seems as animated by issues of salvation and damnation as a medieval morality play, its protagonist is no Everyman. Rather he is what every man who cannot or will not curb his predatory instincts is in danger of becoming. As such, he undergoes a purgatorial ordeal that shapes the novel into a worst-case scenario for modern man.

The rock of purgatory — a barren promontory in mid-Atlantic — supplies the Dantean mise-en-scène for all but the first and last chapters of *Pincher Martin*. Christopher Hadley Martin, a Royal Navy lieutenant during World War II, is

blown off the bridge when his ship is hit by an enemy torpedo. Thrashing about in the water, the drowning man is
apparently saved by his lifebelt and cast ashore on a rock
that miraculously looms up in midocean. There he wages a
desperate struggle for survival punctuated by flashbacks to
episodes in his past that reveal the essential Christopher Martin. Only in the last line of the novel — "You saw the body. He
didn't even have time to kick off his seaboots" — is it made
absolutely clear that Martin has been dead all along. That
Martin's is therefore a metaphysical rather than a physical
ordeal is clarified in Golding's own explication of the novel:

Christopher Hadley Martin had no belief in anything but the importance of his own life; no love, no God. Because he was created
in the image of God, he had a freedom of choice which he used to
centre the world on himself. He did not believe in purgatory and
therefore when he died it was not presented to him in overtly theo-
logical terms. The greed for life which had been the mainspring of
his nature, forced him to refuse the selfless act of dying. He continued to exist in a world composed of his own murderous nature.
His drowned body lies rolling in the Atlantic but the ravenous ego
invents a rock for him to endure on. It is the memory of an aching
tooth. Ostensibly and rationally he is a survivor from a torpedoed
destroyer: but deep down he knows the truth. He is not fighting for
bodily survival but for his continuing identity in the face of what
will smash it and sweep it away — the black lightning, the compassion of God. For Christopher, the Christ-bearer, has become Pincher
Martin who is little but greed. Just to be Pincher is purgatory; to be
Pincher for eternity is hell.[3]

The postmortem drama enacted on the radically circum-
scribed stage of a rock lost in the middle of the Atlantic is
Christopher Martin's valedictory performance. An actor by
profession, he plays in death roles remarkably consistent with
those he played in life. Pete, the producer whose wife Chris
has seduced, insists upon casting him as Greed in a morality play featuring the seven deadly sins: Greed is "simply
you!" While he would hardly be miscast as Pride or Lechery,

Chris is the very incarnation of Greed "who takes anything he can lay his hands on.... He was born with his mouth and his flies open and both hands out to grab." In his omnivorous self-centeredness Chris routinely betrays those around him, reducing people to pawns in a game of ego gratification. His affairs with Sybil, Alfred's girlfriend, and Helen, the producer's wife, seem designed as much to humiliate the men as to seduce the women. When frustrated, Chris becomes aggressive, crippling his friend Peter to retain the lead in a motorcycle race and manhandling Mary Lovell when she resists his sexual advances. After failing to seduce Mary, he thinks of killing her; and later aboard the destroyer only the fatal torpedo prevents him from murdering his only friend, Nat, with whom Mary has fallen in love. Pincher Martin is the conquering hero of Pete's story of the maggots who first eat the fish and then each other, until only one huge all-devouring maggot is left alive. By equating Martin with the maggot that thrives by eating its own kind, Golding employs cannibalism as the ultimate trope of human greed, much as he did in *The Inheritors*.

Of course Martin's greediest ploy of all is his attempt to cheat death by creating his own reality beyond physical extinction. On the invented reality of the rock he erects a stage set for a grandiose solo performance. By endowing each of the rock's prominent features with a local habitation and a name — Oxford Circus, Piccadilly, Leicester Square — Martin invokes the familiar London landmarks that preserve in death the illusion of life. In reconstructing the world he has left behind and in doggedly refusing to give up the struggle to survive, Martin plays the first of his many imaginary roles, that of Robinson Crusoe. Like Defoe's hero, the literary archetype of the castaway, he initially busies himself with the minutiae of survival. So long as he can play the relatively matter-of-fact role of Crusoe, Pincher Martin can concentrate on the specific actions — finding food and water, constructing signals — that may ensure survival and eventual rescue. Again, as in *Lord of the Flies* and *The Inheritors,* Golding parodies an earlier text as a strategy for shedding light on his own. Because Martin's

struggle to endure, unlike Crusoe's, is illusory, no sooner does
Golding's protagonist replicate the tasks associated with the
Crusoe role than he must drop it. No longer able to sustain
his make-believe world as Crusoe, Martin tries on a series of
heroic roles in an increasingly desperate search for an identity
to live by. Each is a projection of an unregenerate ego — all
that remains of Pincher Martin.

In clinging to the imaginary rock of life and refusing to
accept the inalterable fact of his dissolution, Martin continues to defy God in death even as he did in life. "I am Atlas.
I am Prometheus," he cries, invoking the Titans of Greek
mythology who rebelled against the Olympian gods. Both
were punished for their temerity, Atlas by being forced to support the heavens, Prometheus by being chained to the face of
a cliff. Martin's fate is previewed in their unremitting punishments: Atlas can never lay down the heavens; Prometheus
must endure not only bondage but the pain inflicted by an
eagle that tears at his liver for all eternity. Both Titans are associated with rocks, especially Prometheus with whom Martin
more closely identifies. Because Prometheus stole fire to benefit humanity, his defiance of Zeus was as heroic to mortals as
it was blasphemous to the gods. Martin's corresponding defiance of God — "I shit on your heaven!" — is no more than
a vulgar parody of Prometheus's supreme denial of Zeus. Its
futility lies in the devastating irony that the voice shrieking
at God has already been silenced. Equally futile was Martin's
earlier struggle to pile stones at the summit of the rock, an
action that recalls the pointless labors of another mythological figure — Sisyphus. Condemned eternally to roll a heavy
rock up a hill in Hades only to have it roll down again as it
nears the top, Sisyphus, even more than Atlas or Prometheus,
epitomizes Martin's actual condition.

Only under great duress and then only reluctantly does
Pincher Martin abandon the Promethean role of heroic God
defier. That his brief stint as Prometheus is parodic rather than
authentically mimetic is evidenced by its sole result — a successful enema. Martin is no fire stealer bravely asserting an

existential identity in an absurd universe but only a poseur invoking classical roles to shore himself up against impending ruin. His theatrics — accompanied by swelling background music — peak with the enema: "Now I shall be sane and no longer such a slave to my body." But the rejuvenation promised by heroic defecation proves short-lived. It is, ironically, his hard-won sanity that he soon surrenders in a last-ditch effort to ward off the black lightning that will splinter the painted set he has so painstakingly created and with it the "life" he has clung to so tenaciously: "There was still a part that could be played — there was the Bedlamite, Poor Tom, protected from the sign of the black lightning." In Shakespeare's *King Lear,* however, Edgar's role playing results in greater not lesser knowledge. The Duke of Gloucester's legitimate son, Edgar plays the madman to escape the murderous anger engendered in his father by the Machiavellian plotting of the bastard Edmund. As Poor Tom, Edgar, like Martin, feigns madness as a strategy for survival. But innocent Edgar flies from the unrighteous fury of a fallible father while guilty Martin tries to hide from the righteous fury of an infallible God. In his duplicity Martin resembles the God-denying Edmund more than the pious Edgar. Golding, who knows his Shakespeare "pretty well by heart,"[4] may also see in Martin a resemblance to other Shakespearean roleplaying villains. Such dissemblers as Richard III and Iago are self-confessed actors; and Macbeth admits that he plays the king in "borrowed robes." The trope that all the world's a stage and the men and women in it merely players is hardly the exclusive property of Shakespeare's villains. It is, however, they who most frequently hint that the world's perceived insubstantiality excuses a dog-eat-dog morality. Thus invalidated, virtue becomes, in Iago's words, no more than "a fig" — a sentiment no doubt shared by Pincher Martin. Martin emulates an Edmund or an Iago in viewing the world as little better than a staging ground for his self-fashioning theatrics. All resemble actors whose disguises and costume changes are designed to camouflage their darker purposes. As Martin runs out of roles to play, he grows increasingly aware that he is being reduced to a "dark centre." The feigned madness of Poor Tom having proved ineffectual in preserving his dissolving identity, Martin resorts to the real madness of King Lear himself. Reduced to a dark center, bereft of everything but a quacking voice, Martin becomes Golding's parodic version of Lear, mad and naked, reduced by Shakespeare to "unaccommodated man." Scenic and verbal echoes of *King Lear* fill the penultimate chapter of *Pincher Martin,* which opens with a scathing definition of man by Martin that rivals Lear's in its virulence. Lear on his blasted heath and Martin on his barren island rave amidst apocalyptic storms and encroaching darkness. At the height of the storm Martin even misquotes Lear in mimicking the latter's defiance of the raging elements.

   Isolation and divestiture are convenient literary stratagems for investigating human nature. Golding's protagonists, like those in Greek and Shakespearean tragedy, reveal their essential natures most clearly only after being stripped of whatever status protects them from moral scrutiny. The identical process that exposes the self to others may also trigger self-knowledge. Sophocles' Oedipus, blind and powerless, achieves in old age the wisdom that eluded him in his days of glory. And mad Lear and blind Gloucester finally perceive the hitherto elusive truths about their children and themselves. Pincher Martin perceives what he is and why — "Because of what I did I am an outsider and alone" — yet his insight leads not to the redemptive vision of an Oedipus or a Lear but to the threshold of damnation. On the rock, Martin usurps the role of God, parodying the seven days of creation in *Genesis* by forging in the crucible of his ego a world of his own. It is this brave new world in which God is reduced to a bit player fashioned by Martin in his own image that is ultimately shattered by the black lightning. The Pincher Martin who asserts his autonomy even as he is inexorably reduced to a pair of claws never admits the truth of the human condition Golding represents in the tiny glass figure floating upright in a jam jar. Man is no more autonomous in the sight of God than is the glass figure in the sight of man: "You could let it struggle towards the surface, give it almost a bit of air then send it steadily, slowly, remorselessly down and down."

Martin's imaginary landscape illustrates Golding's belief that it is man's nature "to make the universe in the image of his own mind."[5] Even as his self-created universe crumbles around him Martin recapitulates the turning away from God that had been his habit since childhood. In his autobiographical essay, "The Ladder and the Tree," Golding recounts his own recurrent nightmare that "became a convenient metaphor for the experience of the human being turning away from God and into egotism, the darkness of egotism."[6] The "looming terror which I knew night-long in my very bones"[7] surfaces in Martin's memory of the "cellar door swinging to behind a small child who must go down, down in his sleep to meet the thing he turned from when he was created." The "thing," of course, is God whose presence Martin has denied for a lifetime.

What terrifies Martin into his last and most desperate evasive posture — the role of mad Lear — is the sudden appearance of an old woman. This specter, who had lurked in the darkest corner of the cellar/psyche, confined by the repressive power of Martin's ego, is now "loose on the rock ... out of the cellar and in daylight." The collapse of Martin's psyche is evidenced by his futile slashing away at her evanescent form no knife can penetrate. Now implacably in the foreground of his consciousness, knowledge, embodied in the old woman, can no longer be suppressed. Given the bizarre scenario that follows her appearance, the old woman functions as Golding's version of the Angel of the Annunciation. For the "hallucination" that replaces her and that proceeds to enact with Martin the finale of his self-fashioned drama is none other than God himself. Because the apparition seated before him is dressed as a sailor, Martin is able momentarily to regard it as a projection of his own mind. Not even when the rock is revealed to be "like cardboard, a painted flat" does Martin completely abandon the fiction that he created God rather than vice versa. But neither the "blurred window" of his perception nor the claim of madness — "Even that crevice will crumble," retorts the spectral sailor — suffice any longer to preserve his version of reality. Martin has at last come face-to-face with the ultimate reality that confounds and negates his own.

God's immanence and the colloquy He carries on with Martin manifest the grace He extends even to the most hardened sinner. Martin must freely surrender the distorted identity he has created and nurtured in defiance of God. Although his earlier admission of guilt — "Because of what I did I am an outsider and alone" — seemed to signal the contrition that initiates redemption, Martin refuses to go further. To take the next step would mean surrendering the "life" he has manufactured after death. Golding casts the colloquy between Martin and God in the form of a catechism in which God's questions are designed to pry Martin loose from the rock of his ego. Implicit in God's "Consider now," repeated after Martin's every refusal, is His infinite compassion. Martin's reply is to hold out his identity disc — badge of the unregenerate self — while screaming at God, "I spit on your compassion!" Even when a mouth no longer exists, a disembodied voice issuing from the "centre" of what was once Pincher Martin shrieks his last defiant words: "I shit on your heaven!" By rejecting God's heaven for his own hell, Martin plumbs the depths of obduracy. Although the purgatorial ordeal he has undergone ostensibly prepares the sinner for heaven, Martin's fate is by no means certain. Golding's remark that "to be Pincher for eternity is hell" seems to subvert the traditional Christian notion of purgatory as a way station to heaven. The blackness of the lightning that closes in on Martin, finally blasting away his identity, corresponds to the blackness of his soul. Analogous to the darkness of the cellar that reflects the darkness within, the black lightning symptomizes Martin's rejection of God. Presumably white lightning is reserved for those who accept God as light, black lightning for those who relegate God to darkness. That the light stalking Martin is black may therefore be the best evidence that Golding consigns him permanently to hell.

If the purgatorial ordeal leads Martin not to heaven but to hell, then he suffers a double dying — after his ship is torpedoed and again after he rejects God's grace. The title of the first American edition — *The Two Deaths of Christopher Martin* (1957) — while never authorized by Golding — nonetheless calls attention to the metaphorical second dying that turns out to be Martin's "real" death. That this second death is tantamount to damnation may be read in God's silence after Martin opts for his own version of creation. Despite God's warning that the "crevice of madness" into which Martin creeps as King Lear will crumble like his previous defenses, Martin refuses to retract the doomsday scenario he has scripted for himself. Apropos of the black lightning that reveals the rock "to be as insubstantial as the painted water" all that remains of Pincher (pincer?) Martin is a pair of claws surrounded by "an island of papery stuff." In this final incarnation Martin completes in death a Dantean metamorphosis into the ultimate symbol of what he was in life. Yet as startling as is Martin's transformation, it is primarily a testament not to change but to stasis. To really change is to become no longer himself — precisely what Martin is unwilling and/or unable to achieve. Changelessness reflects that persistence in error that consigns sinners to hell. Martin resembles the sinners in Dante's *Inferno* whose placement, personification, and punishment in hell are all determined by the contours of their earthly lives. Simple greed, such as the gluttony of Ciacco the Hog, warrants comparatively light punishment in the upper reaches of hell. Greed as voracious as Martin's, however, which damages, even destroys, the lives of others, reaps far graver consequences than that of Ciacco whose unseemly abuse of food and drink harmed chiefly himself. Martin's reduction to a pair of lobster claws parallels the metamorphic distortions suffered in the bowels of hell by those sinners who did violence to others or to God. Helpless to maintain a stable form, their constant transformations in death reflect their duplicitous conduct in life. Like theirs, Martin's many identities add up to none. All pervert human nature by distorting it to serve their ends. To the religious imagination the ultimate perversion consists of turning away from God. Bernard Dick argues that in defying God Martin reenacts the blasphemy of Capaneus whom Dante punishes in the seventh circle of hell as one of the violent against God. Capaneus boasted that even Zeus could not prevent him from scaling the walls of Thebes. Zeus answered this blasphemy "by striking him dead with a thunderbolt which, according to Statius who recounts the incident in *The Thebiad,* left his shield blackened — perhaps the source of Golding's black lightning."[8]

The more immediate source of the all-consuming black lightning in *Pincher Martin* is Nathaniel Walterson who employs it as a metaphor for the nothingness that may await those who are unprepared for death: "Take us as we are now and heaven would be sheer negation. Without form and void. You see? A sort of black lightning destroying everything that we call life." Nat, Chris's only true friend, is a character type that recurs in most of Golding's novels and that first appears as Simon in *Lord of the Flies.* Like Simon, Nat is one of Golding's saints who stands for the moral order and against the predominant bleakness of the human condition. Nat's religiosity takes the form of an intuitive knowledge that in its prescience — he foresees Chris's imminent death — suggests a divine origin. Indeed, his cautionary lecture to Chris, which Nat calls "a talk on the technique of dying," previews God's advice in chapter 13. Nat, like Christ, mediates between God and man, teaching by his own example the renunciation of the world that eases the acceptance of death. Martin's drowning screams for help juxtapose the two: "Nat! Nathaniel! For Christ's sake! Nathaniel! Help!" In time-honored religious fashion, Nat hopes to effect in Chris the necessary change of heart by invoking the certainty of death. The warning instills the requisite terror but not its positive consequence. What terrifies Chris is not the prospect of heaven as "sheer negation" but the egregious reminder of his own mortality. Even more terrifying is Nat's forecast of death "in only a few years." Designed to impress upon his friend the urgency of preparing himself to "achieve heaven," Nat's dire prediction has the opposite effect. Too devoted to this world to concern himself about heaven, Chris reacts by clinging even more tenaciously to the only reality he admits. The conversation between Nat and Chris underscores their polar opposition in the symbolic design of *Pincher Martin:* the former incarnates the best in man, the latter the worst.

Turning away from Nat and the prospect of salvation he holds out, Martin rehearses his later turning away from God. Nat's exhortation to surrender this world in preparation for the next is a preliminary version of God's attempt to pry Martin loose from his illusory rock. In rebuffing Nat, Martin considers himself the worldly-wise man, Nat the "awful bloody fool"; in rebuffing God he casts himself as the heroic loner (Atlas, Prometheus), God as the "great bloody bully." Whatever his imagined role, however, Martin seems actually to be reenacting a master plot that is as old as Western literature. *Pincher Martin* is a modern adaptation of the traditional story whose protagonist is forced to choose between salvation and damnation. Invariably the hero must understand the consequences of his choice: heaven or hell. Medieval drama, which consists of little else but the conflict between good and evil implicit in the heaven or hell scenario, is inhabited by all sorts of good angels whose chief role it is to inform the hero of the various risks to his immortal soul. Nat is, of course, the good angel of *Pincher Martin,* invoking imminent death and warning of its aftermath in time-honored fashion. Nat's black lightning is one of those horrifying damnation metaphors — like the more familiar fiery pit — which are intended to jar the sinner from his evil ways and set him on the path to redemption. Martin's rejection is as typical as Nat's warning. Rarely does the sinner instantly reform; the greater part of his story dramatizes his doubt, vacillation, backsliding, etc. Often his fate is held in suspense until the end, as in Marlow's *Dr. Faustus* when the protagonist facing death is confronted one last time by the representatives of good and evil. A similar eleventh-hour reprieve is offered Martin when God appears in chapter 13 to beg him to consider. And the black lightning, formerly a symbol of annihilation but now its instrument, is invoked to make visible and unmistakable the awful wages of sin. Yet so intransigent is Martin that neither love (God's patience) nor fear (black lightning), the traditional spurs to repentance, suffices to save him from himself.

Whatever the hero's fate, he chooses it. God is invariably compassionate, amazingly so in Martin's case. In fact, Martin's double dying illustrates not only how tenacious is his greedy hold on life but also how God in His infinite mercy grants him an unprecedented second chance to "consider." Given that Martin dies at the beginning of the novel, what follows on the rock (i.e., all but the first and last chapters) epitomizes God's boundless compassion no less than Martin's boundless egotism. Since the theology of *Pincher Martin* is traditionally Christian in the depiction of an omnipotent Creator, Martin's second "life" on the rock may be interpreted as a prolongation of his "final" death by an all-merciful God bent on saving even so blackened a soul. That Martin is aware of the double dying phenomenon is implicit at the beginning of chapter 12 when, anxious to "protect normality," he expresses fear of annihilation: "I don't want to die again." At the same time he feels himself being "squeezed thin" and his features being distorted. Martin's marred profile — a suddenly elongated mouth, two noses — testifies to his inability to preserve the outward form of normality. Like Dante's thieves in the eighth circle of *Inferno* whose bodies are being constantly taken from them, Martin is manipulated in death as he manipulated others in life. Among the thieves is the unregenerate Vanni Fucci whose obscene gesture at God evidences an arrogance toward God that surpasses even that of Capaneus. Martin's "I shit on your heaven!" replicates the moral degeneracy of Dante's greatest blasphemer: like Fucci in hell, Martin on his rock chooses to defy God and perseveres in his defiance no matter how futile and painful its consequences.

The blasphemy of a Fucci or a Capaneus — or a Christopher Martin — demonstrates free will at its most perverse. Yet the existence of free will is no less crucial to *Pincher Martin* than to the *Inferno*. Golding's theology is grounded in

the proposition that man has free will because he was created in God's image, that he had free will the way God has it. Well, once you have free will and you are created, you have alternatives before you. You can either turn towards God or away from Him. And God can't stop you turning away from Him without removing your free will, because that's what free will is. This is the whole thing about *Pincher Martin*. It's that and nothing else. When you turn away from God, He becomes a darkness; when you turn towards Him, He becomes a light, in cliché terms.[9]

Symptomatic of the misuse of free will that leads Martin not toward but away from God is his incapacity to imagine a being greater than himself. Six days into his parody of *Genesis*, Martin yells at the sailor opposite him: "On the sixth day he created God. Therefore I permit you to use nothing but my own vocabulary. In his own image created he Him." In the form of the sailor Martin has indeed created God in his own image down to the features, the clothing, the seaboots. Forever greedy he insists to the end on his "own vocabulary" that creates in the mirror image of the sailor an equal adversary. That Martin is able to incarnate God solely in the sailor/self is à priori evidence of a fatal predisposition if not predestination.

God asks of Martin that he surrender his self-fashioned identity as Pincher, the Maggot for the identity that embodies the reality of the human condition: that of the figure floating in the jam jar. To do so Martin must jettison his concept of the indispensable centrality of the self that relegates even God to a "projection of my mind." Playing Atlas and Prometheus (and Capaneus for that matter) simply recapitulates their error, distorting in the service of a bogus heroism the true relationship between man and God. A better role model is Oedipus who learned by suffering to bend his will to God's and thus find peace in a rectified image of the universe. What is required of Martin is therefore clear. But what if his grasping nature is itself created by God? Without misreading his rejection of God's terms as justifiable much less heroic, it is still possible to consider Martin's rejoinder: "Yet, suppose I climbed away from the cellar over the bodies of used and defeated people, broke them to make steps on the road away from you, why should you torture me? If I ate them, who gave me a mouth?" At first glance, Martin seems merely to be blaming his own shortcomings on God. Yet his specific accusation that God has stacked the deck by creating in him the maggot's all-devouring predisposition is not entirely frivolous. Martin argues that he is being unjustly punished for the evil that was genetically encoded by God. Given his inherent nature, how could he be expected to exercise free will except to nurture the maggot within?

The uselessness of Martin's question is revealed in God's reply: "There is no answer in your vocabulary." God's design, in other words, is not susceptible to man's interpretation. By insisting on his own vocabulary Martin attempts to cast God as a rival debater in a Promethean scenario. It is again a measure of God's compassion that He temporarily accepts this role in the hope of effecting a change of heart in the obdurate Martin. Far from persecuting him, God favors Martin by assuming the only form that has the potential of closing the distance between them. As Martin's sailor/self God extends to the unregenerate sinner an eleventh-hour offer of reprieve in the only identity and in the only vocabulary that Martin can understand. Because he is plainly incapable of the leap of faith enjoined by Nat and conventionally required for redemption, Martin is asked by God only to let go voluntarily of the manifestly "cardboard" set he has created. But, marooned on the rock of his own ego, the endlessly recalcitrant sinner clings to it all the more tenaciously by invoking those dramatic personae (Atlas, Prometheus) whose radical self-assertions parallel his own "I am! I am! I am!" In responding to God's injunctions to surrender the self with ever more desperate strategies to sustain it, Martin ironically strips himself of the very defenses that his invented personae were invoked to fortify. From the moment when God the sailor appears to ask whether he has "had enough," Martin can evade the dreaded black lightning only by surrender. It is no accident that his defiance coincides with the disappearance of the sailor and the spread of the lightning. In a fatal metamorphosis that trivializes Martin's roleplaying, the solicitous sailor becomes the black lightning of annihilation.

A complementary transformation occurs when the no-longer-to-be-evaded black lightning exposes the world of Martin's creation: "The sea stopped moving, froze, became paper. . . . The rock was painted on the same paper." Martin had perceived lightning and sea working in tandem to create the storm scene of his final ravings as mad Lear. Like everything and everyone else, God included, even the atavistic sea had been subsumed and exploited by Martin's omnivorous ego. The dissociation of the black lightning from the sea signals the dissolution of his cardboard world. Freezing the roiling sea of Martin's imagination, the black lightning destroys — as Nat had warned — "everything that we call life."

In traditional Christianity the purgatorial ordeal culminates with the soul's release into heaven. Martin would be saved *malgré lui,* his blasphemies ignored or forgiven by a God of love whose compassion is as infinite as it is inscrutable. The meaning of the purgatorial experience lies in its efficacy in cleansing the blackened soul of even the most persistent sinner. If a Pincher Martin — the epitome of human evil — can be redeemed, then the very implausibility of his salvation would testify to the limitless compassion of God. Questioned about the reality of purgatory as a place in which we learn to "die into heaven" Golding is skeptical: "I hope devoutly that there is no survival after death." Given human nature, its endless extension would be "pointless:" a "really merciful God would destroy" His creation after its allotted life span. Although Christopher Martin is not Everyman, he nevertheless embodies, albeit in monstrous form, the bleak reality of the human condition. "And, of course, if he changes into some other creature, if the spark of God, which is said to lie in every man, if that returns to God, well, it's so unlike the creature it inhabited that you might as well say there's no survival after death."[10]

The issue of survival after death is similarly raised on the last page of *Pincher Martin* by Mr. Campbell who twice alludes to the "sad harvest" of Martin's remains, which he has discovered and which Mr. Davidson, the naval officer, has arrived to claim. Reminiscent of the "gimmicked" conclusion of *Lord of the Flies,* the final chapter of *Pincher Martin* is no more sanguine about the human condition. Like the callow officer of *Lord of the Flies,* the matter-of-fact Mr. Davidson can apprehend only what is most obvious. He can reply to Mr. Campbell's anguished, "Would you say there was any — surviving? Or is that all?" simply by calling attention to the seaboots that Martin never kicked off as evidence that he hadn't "suffered." The many ambiguities of "suffered" are thus evoked by Mr. Campbell's unanswered — and unanswerable — question. Little more than Mr. Davidson's clumsy solace seems warranted by the "wreck" of Martin's body. "Broken, defiled," that body had been wearing away like the pair of lobster claws to which Martin had been symbolically reduced. It is God's black lightning playing over the claws, "prying for a weakness, wearing them away in a compassion that was timeless and without mercy," that may promise the total obliteration that in Golding's view the "creature" that is man has earned. The final death of the claws that Martin has become need presage neither heaven nor hell. For the claws exist chiefly as a macabre memento mori — a token of the evil in man that only his destruction can eradicate.

5

Cosmic Chaos: *Free Fall*

Sammy Mountjoy, the hero of *Free Fall* (1959), has "hung all systems on the wall like a row of useless hats." An artist good enough to "hang in the Tate," Sammy is in search of an all-encompassing pattern that not even his art is able to impress upon life. His is the dilemma of Golding's "model intellectual of the twentieth century" whose "particular poignancy" derives from his inability to commit himself to any system of values. "Where for hundreds of thousands of years men have known where they were, now they don't know where they are any longer. This is the point of *Free Fall*."[1] Without a "codified morality" man is "like a creature in space, tumbling, eternally tumbling, no up, no down, just in 'free fall' in the scientific sense."[2] In seeking a "hat" of his own that will at least hint at an acceptable pattern, Sammy begins by rejecting the "rationalist hat" that makes man the measure of all things. Implied in Sammy's refusal "to confuse our limitations with the bounds of possibility" is Golding's belief that it is science itself that induces the state of free fall by sweeping away old systems. *Free Fall* thus evokes in the scientific metaphor of Golding's title both the quintessential condition of modern man and its genesis. Sammy begins where many pattern seekers in modern fiction end: with the conviction that any neat scheme is inadequate and that only "cosmic chaos" lies behind it. A first-person narrator "translating incoherence into incoherence," Sammy Mountjoy is Golding's representative modern man whose story illustrates "the patternlessness of life before we impose any patterns on it." What Sammy hopes to find out is how to resolve the basic problem of modern man: "learning to live fearlessly with the natural chaos of existence, without forcing artificial patterns on it."[3]

Sammy's attempt to make sense of "the natural chaos of existence" is triggered by a crisis of despair. Via his retrospective narrative he hopes to pinpoint that critical moment of "the decision made freely that cost me my freedom." The personal hell out of which he writes — "the monstrous world of my present consciousness" — began at the precise moment when freedom was lost. In sifting the minutiae of his life for the all-important clue to his present malaise, Sammy asks after each recollected episode, "Here?" *Free Fall* becomes a sort of detective story in which various pieces of evidence are examined and discarded until the mystery is solved. Central to Sammy's investigative narrative is its presumptive linkage of self-created hell with lost freedom. In Sammy's obsession with freedom Golding fictionalizes his own: "But I was concerned very much with the question of freedom of action, and I finally found I couldn't explain this in any way."[4] The result — *Free Fall* — is an autobiographical inversion that is reminiscent of the textual inversions of the earlier novels. Because Golding considered his own life "hideously respectable," he required a protagonist of dissimilar background (illegitimate birth, slum childhood, patchy education) but of certain crucial common experiences (artistic vocation, wartime service, postwar angst).

Although Golding may have conceived the novel as inverted autobiography and eschewed his usual reversal of a specific text, *Free Fall* no more exists in a literary vacuum than does *Lord of the Flies* or *The Inheritors*. In its obsession with freedom, *Free Fall* mirrors the transcendent issue of existentialist literature. Existentialist characters invariably concern themselves with the problem of identity. Sammy Mountjoy's attempt to identify that moment when he lost his freedom is equally an attempt to identify what he is in terms of what he was. Although Golding's essentially religious view of the universe and of man's place in it clashes with the existentialist tenet that man and his position in the universe are fundamentally absurd, his concession that "my generation is an existentialist generation" admits points of correspondence.[5] Golding would, for example, agree with those existentialists who recoil from rationalism, insisting on the limits of reason even as they acknowledge its primacy. Not only in trying to make sense of the present by evoking memories of the past but in employing reason to do so, Sammy acts as an existentialist. And in existentialist fashion he discovers the failure of rationalism to provide a viable moral system. Golding's own flight from the nineteenth-century rationalism epitomized by his father parallels Sammy's ultimate rejection of the rationalist philosophy of Nick Shales. But the existentialist echoes in *Free Fall* are confined neither to problems of freedom and identity nor to matters of philosophical speculation. Setting aside the question of whether Golding has written an existentialist novel or a parody of one, it is difficult to read *Free Fall* without recalling two French existentialist classics: Jean-Paul Sartre's *Nausea* (1938) and Albert Camus's *The Fall* (1956).

Sammy Mountjoy's crisis of despair and its symptoms — self-doubt, metaphysical anguish — resemble Antoine Roquentin's in *Nausea*. Disgusted with his existence, Roquentin has arrived at the same impasse that confronts Sammy whose decision to disinter the past originates in a similar malaise. They also share a nearly palpable loneliness derived in part from a felt disjunction between themselves and others, even between themselves and their surroundings. Rotten Row, in English towns something of a generic name for the sort of slum street where Sammy spent his childhood, evokes a world as ugly as Roquentin's Bouville. Sartre's title refers to the nausea that symptomizes Roquentin's constant revulsion from the filth and squalor that is similarly evoked in the cloacal imagery of *Free Fall*. Sammy's grotesque mother, seated symbolically on a toilet; the neighborhood gamine, Evie; the retarded Minnie; and the ruined Beatrice, all of whom characteristically urinate in front of Sammy, might as easily inhabit Roquentin's "gross" world of "rotten filth" forever sticking to him. *Free*

Fall and *Nausea* alike feature a first-person narrator of artistic sensibility living through an identity crisis at a high pitch of metaphysical intensity. Sartre's dictum that "life begins on the other side of despair" applies equally to Sammy and Roquentin. Both embody the *mauvaise foi* (bad faith) that for Sartre characterizes the guilty actions of modern man. Given the guilty past, anguished present, and uncertain future of its quintessential protagonist, an existentialist novel tends to end inconclusively. Tentative outcomes are themselves reflections of a philosophy grounded in man's ability endlessly to re-create himself. Beyond despair lies not the finality of being but the fluidity of becoming, a process concluded only by the contingency of death.

The many outward resemblances between *Free Fall* and *Nausea* suggest that Golding may have written an unintentionally existentialist novel. Yet the obsession with freedom that empowers both novels results in conclusions that, while similarly tenuous, are otherwise divergent. At the end of *Nausea* Roquentin, having rejected the detritus of the past (including his own former selves), stands poised to achieve an existential breakthrough. Reduced to nothing, he intuits in a snatch of jazz the way out of his dilemma: if he can create — albeit in words rather than in music — a valid work of art, then perhaps he will be able to remember his life "without repugnance." A finished book would fulfill the existentialist ideal of commitment, simultaneously clarifying the past and validating the reestablished self. Nothing is settled at the end of *Nausea*: in concrete terms Roquentin has done no more than approach the point of departure. Sammy's fate is equally uncertain. He, too, had sought a point of departure; but in his case the search was for the point where he lost his freedom, not for the point where he might regain or achieve it. For Sammy — and for Golding — the past cannot be transformed or canceled as it is in *Nausea*. Nor can art provide the solace it promises for Roquentin; Sammy is already a famous painter. It is finally Golding's Christianity — grounded in the doctrine of Original Sin — that separates him from Sartre.

The endless refashioning of the self — de rigueur for existentialists — is anathema to Golding and results in a Pincher Martin. Unlike Martin whose evil he recapitulates in consciously and callously manipulating and betraying Beatrice, Sammy is redeemable precisely because he accepts his guilt by refusing to negate the past. At the end of *Free Fall* Sammy has succeeded in pinpointing the moment when, frantic to possess Beatrice and careless of the consequences, he lost his freedom. While his redemption is no more guaranteed than Roquentin's, Sammy has at least avoided compounding his sin by trying to purchase freedom with selective amnesia.

If Golding is rewriting the existentialist novel in *Free Fall* as he rewrote the boy's adventure story in *Lord of the Flies* and evolutionary theory in *The Inheritors,* then Camus's *The Fall* is the subverted text. Published and translated into English only three years prior to *Free Fall, The Fall* may itself owe something to *Nausea.* All three novels are first-person confessions designed to investigate the existence and exercise of free will. In one sense or another all three protagonists have fallen; but Sammy emulates Camus's Jean-Baptiste Clamence in focusing his attention on the exact moment of his fall. The titles, the autobiographical surveys, the delayed revelations of the point of no return, and the linkage between a woman's fall and the protagonist's are among the many congruities of *Free Fall* and *The Fall.* Clamence dates his fall from an act of omission, not, like Sammy, from an act of commission. From the moment when he neglected to dive into the Seine in an attempt to save a suicidal woman from drowning Clamence has been haunted by his failure of nerve. In that critical moment of inaction Clamence's fate was sealed: like the drowned woman, he falls into water, in his case from the paradise of Paris into the watery milieu of Amsterdam whose canals he likens to the concentric circles of hell. Sammy lives on Paradise Hill, ostensibly a world removed from the Rotten Row of his origins; but like Clamence he actually exists in a personal hell compounded of his own guilt. His visit to the madhouse where he encounters the vegetative remains of Beatrice parallels Clamence's wished-for second chance to save the drowning woman. It is too late for Beatrice and the anonymous suicide — and for their would-be saviours. Clamence's "It will always be too late" concedes the impossibility of altering the past and, perhaps, of altering himself. His devastating conclusion implies that even given a chance to revise the past, the guilty man is just as likely to repeat it. Conceivably, the worldly Clamence's cynical view of man is the existentialist version of original sin. What Clamence abstracts from his own life — universal human guilt — is implicit in Sammy's. Despite a surname that suggests forgiveness (*clémence*) Camus's protagonist offers no hope of redemption. Man's fate is symbolized in Clamence's reference to the medieval little-ease, a cell "not high enough to stand up in nor yet wide enough to lie down in." Like the broom closet in which as a prisoner of war (Clamence, incidentally, spent time in a German internment camp) Sammy was briefly confined by the sinister Dr. Halde, the little-ease represents the "unchanging restriction" that Clamence assigns to the guilt-ridden human condition. That Clamence's trope relates as well to Sammy is clarified in the latter's first impressions of his "cell." Groping blindfolded amidst darkness (another index of the human condition?) Sammy imagines having to "keep lifting my chin in order to look over" the "likeness of a wall"; and "dungeon stories flew through my head, oubliettes, walls that moved, the little-ease."

Still, despite this most unmistakable echo of Camus, Golding's is not the absurd universe of the existentialists. As usual, he subsumes competing ideologies within an essentially traditional Christian context. It is not so much that the existentialist view is invalid as that it is inadequate. Like the rationalism of Nick Shales, existentialism fails to take into account the religious dimension of human experience as represented, albeit imperfectly and ironically, by Rowena Pringle in *Free Fall*. So petty and spiteful is Miss Pringle, the religion teacher, and so selfless and solicitous is Nick, the science teacher, that Sammy rejects her "Moses and Jehovah" for his rationalism. The two teachers incarnate the opposing values that Sammy encounters in other similarly paired characters: honest Johnny Spragg and treacherous Philip Arnold; innocent Beatrice and sophisticated Taffy. What Sammy eventually discovers is that the natural and spiritual worlds exist "side by side." Seemingly opposed, existentialism and rationalism alike reflect materialism — a partial ontology at best. Sammy's cry of "Help me! Help me!" can only be raised to God. Although he recalls it as no more than the "instinctive" cry "of the rat when the terrier shakes it," Sammy understands that "the very act of crying out changed the thing that cried." That man is capable of change evidences at least his redeemability if not his actual redemption. A "search for a place where help may be found," Sammy's cry is an implicit affirmation of the spiritual dimension that he had suppressed. It is this spiritual burst through the metaphorical door of the self that leads to the opening of the real door of the cell. And the revelation that the cell is only a broom closet and that what Sammy took for a severed penis is only a damp rag effectively subverts the physical "evidence" and spotlights the inadequacy of any exclusively materialistic worldview. Sprung from the traps of cell and self, Sammy is at last able to perceive in the disparate aspects of human experience the outline of a moral order. In so doing he transcends Jean-Baptiste Clamence's sardonic one-sentence summary of modern man: "he fornicated and read the papers."

In denying Clamence the last word on man, *Free Fall* is revealed as a critique rather than an embodiment of the existentialist novel. What Sammy's rationalism is to his personal narrative, existentialism is to Golding's overall design. Both rationalism and existentialism function primarily to expose the shortcomings of materialistic systems. In *Free Fall* competing ideologies are accommodated in order finally to subsume them under the rubric of Christianity. Arguably religious, Sammy's quest is conducted essentially along Dantean lines; and its ultimate meaning owes more to *La Vita Nuova* (The new life) and the *Divine Comedy* than to any existentialist text. *Free Fall* opens at the same crisis point reached by Dante at the outset of *Inferno*. Midway through life's journey Dante is stricken by the realization that he has strayed from the path of virtue into the Dark Wood of Error. At once he lifts his eyes to a hill — the Mount of Joy — bathed in the light of divine illumination. But his ascent is blocked by three beasts of worldliness, and he is driven back into the darkness of error. At this point the shade of Virgil (Human Reason) appears, explaining that he has been sent to rescue Dante from error and that only by first descending into Hell (recognizing sin) and then ascending through Purgatory (renouncing sin) can Paradise (the pinnacle of joy and the light of God) be attained. In the first several pages of *Free Fall* Sammy Mountjoy alludes repeatedly to the darkness that "sits" at his "centre"; once a "little boy, clear as spring water," he has become a "man like a stagnant pool." His decision to find out where he went astray by submerging himself in his past parallels Dante's descent into hell. Essentially a rationalist despite his disavowal of all systems, Sammy employs reason to survey his life for the critical moment of loss just as Dante depends upon reason in the person of Virgil to guide his descent into hell. Even when the texture of *Free Fall* is not recognizably Dantean it is nonetheless pervasively religious: Sammy's mother prefers to identify his unknown father as a churchman; Sammy's is the "world of sin and redemption." And words such as *salvation, redemption, resurrected,* and *transfigured* constantly reaffirm the spiritual nature of Sammy's quest.

One critic goes so far as to see in *Free Fall* a microcosm of the entire *Divine Comedy,* citing the "linear development of the novel's Dantean parallel from *Inferno* (chapter 9) through *Purgatorio* (10) and *Paradise* (13)."[6] Thus hell is the closet cell where Sammy's fear for his "privates" turns a scrap of cloth into a severed penis. That his hell is evoked in sexual terms recalls the sin that cost Sammy his freedom. As in the *Inferno,* the punishment reflects the sin. Up to this point only Sammy's guilty conscience distinguishes him from Pincher Martin. In fact the sexual voracity that characterizes them both has graver consequences for Beatrice, the girl Sammy exploits, than it does for Mary, the equally innocent girl Martin attacks. It is Sammy's cry — to a God denied by Martin — that provisionally spares the one the fate of the other. The camp commandant as deus ex machina restores the contrite Sammy to life, releasing him from the physical torment that is intensified for the recalcitrant Martin by God the sailor. Whether hell is represented in the dark closet cell of chapter 9 and purgatory in the open air of the prison camp in chapter 10, or an extended purgatorial experience is represented in the two chapters taken together, the wartime segments of Sammy's narrative assume a Dantean pattern. When, for example, Sammy emerges from darkness into light he is "a man resurrected but not by him" (i.e., the commandant). The huts of the prison camp "shone with the innocent light of their own created nature" in a newly pristine world. A fellow officer becomes "a being of great glory" to a reborn Sammy who has gained a "complete and luminous sanity" that pierces the veil of appearance to apprehend a world of radiant beauty. Visited "by a flake of fire, miraculous and pentecostal, ... transmuted ... once and forever," he achieves a Dantean vision of paradise regained. After the war, Sammy returns to England where he lives on Paradise Hill. Although Golding's usual inconclusive ending makes it unclear whether like Dante Sammy can win the real *Paradiso,* it is certain that only via the purgatorial ordeal of the prison camp may paradise be won.

If for Sammy paradise proves unattainable it is because the gravity of the evil he so painstakingly traces back to its source defies redemption. Dante's *Inferno* is filled with sinners whose specific evils apparently warrant automatic damnation. Most unforgivable are those acts that are evil not only in their results but in their inceptions. Dante distinguishes between sins of passion (especially those involving love) and sins of premeditation, reserving the severest punishments for the latter. Although Sammy's youthful passion for Beatrice is conceived in love, it is achieved in duplicity. On his graduation day — a symbolic crossroads — he makes the crucial decision that propels him into free fall. In an interior monologue that parodies the catechism Sammy asks himself, "What will you sacrifice?" to possess Beatrice. The answer — "Everything" — might just as easily have come from Pincher Martin and all but invites damnation. His decision to risk all for earthly lust is itself a parody of Dante's decision — reflected in his voluntary and hazardous descent into hell — to risk all for heavenly love. Of course, the entirety of Sammy's self-analyzing narrative can be read as a parody of Dante. This is especially true of the Beatrice episodes that largely subvert or negate corresponding episodes in the *Divine Comedy* and *La Vita Nuova*.

Dante's blessed Beatrice is a divine intercessor whose spotless life is rewarded by the early death that justly removes her to heaven. From on high she watches over the steadfastly faithful Dante whom she will meet again in heaven, thus to lead him ever upwards toward God. *La Vita Nuova* records, then, the successive stages of Dante's devotion to — or worship of — an exalted being, a tutelary spirit who becomes the instrument of his salvation in the *Divine Comedy*. At first Sammy regards Beatrice Ifor with the same awe that inspired Dante's devotion. A chapel dominates the South London neighborhood where men "were privileged to live in this land touched by the feet of Beatrice." The lovesick Sammy imagines asking a passerby in some remote corner of the world for news of Beatrice — whether, for example, she has been "canonized by the Catholic church." Key stages of his early pursuit of her parallel scenes in *La Vita Nuova*. Sammy arranges to meet Beatrice "accidentally" as she leaves her training college accompanied by two "blessed damozels," evoking Dante's unexpected sight of his Beatrice walking with two women down a Florentine street. The staged meeting is a subversion of the spontaneous one — and a rehearsal for the many manipulative tactics Sammy later employs. Shortly thereafter he declares his love in a maudlin letter ("my bourgeois pamphlet"), a hopeless parody of the lovely ballad in which Dante addresses his love to Beatrice in *La Vita Nuova*. A particularly powerful evocation of *La*

Vita Nuova occurs when the lovers approach a similarly critical moment in their relationships. Walking in the country
beside a pure stream inspires Dante to cast off despair and to
achieve new heights of devotion. Immediately after the headmaster advises him that anything can be had "providing you
are willing to make the appropriate sacrifice," Sammy walks
through a forest from which he emerges to swim in "provi-
dential waters." As though baptized anew he feels "healed"
by the waters. Remembering the headmaster's advice but discounting his prophetic warning that "the sacrifice is always
regretted," Sammy now makes the fatal decision — to sacrifice
everything to possess Beatrice — that costs him his freedom.

It is at this point that Sammy's love diverges once and for
all from its Dantean prototype. The sexual implications of
Sammy's decision convert Beatrice Ifor (If/or) — the "blessed"
girl radiant in "the light round her brow of paradise" — into a
sexual object. For Dante's ideal human love, the sublunary approximation of the divine love of God, Sammy substitutes "the
tickling pleasure" of sexual gratification. The desecration of
Beatrice's nunlike innocence reenacts his boyhood defilement
of the church altar and is conceived in similar terms. Thus
sexual consummation is equated by Sammy with "the altar of
whatever shoddy temple was left to us." Whereas Dante's ideal
love pointed the way to heaven, Sammy's debased love exposes
the route to hell. Not long after he brings Beatrice "into the
sexual orbit" Sammy arrives at "the knowledge that if this
was everything it was a poor return for birth." Predictably,
the innocent and religious Beatrice proves unresponsive, their
one-sided lovemaking a sordid sexual exploitation. Her pas-
sivity drives Sammy to ever more flagrant acts of sexual abuse,
all of which she accepts submissively. What he envisioned as a
love that would raise his life to the "holy level of hers" turns
out to be an "infliction," an emblem of his "own degradation." The more degrading her exploitation, the more devoted
her love: after an act that fills him with "self-contempt" she
looks "as though she had been blessed." This ironic perversion
of the formerly straightforward religious imagery surround-

ing Beatrice culminates in Sammy's remembrance that "there was no light in her face" shortly after he takes up with Taffy. In his dream water rises around the deserted Beatrice who runs crying out after his receding form. The rising water that overtakes her but that cannot reach him hauntingly evokes the moment of *mauvaise foi* when Jean-Baptiste Clamence ignored the drowning woman in *The Fall.*

The dream of rising water becomes a reality in the sanatorium where the nearly subhuman Beatrice, unable to recognize Sammy, urinates on the floor and over his shoes. Seven years elapse between Dante's second encounter with his Beatrice and her death, approximately the time that passes between Sammy's dream and its symbolic enactment. In the radically different fates of the two Beatrices lies the difference between sacred and profane love. Dante's love translates Beatrice into heaven and eternal life; Sammy's reduces Beatrice Ifor to animal status and living death. As a boy Sammy had explored with Johnny Spragg the grounds of this very lunatic asylum, "wandering in paradise" through the gardens of what was then a "magic house." Arriving at the converted mansion to visit Beatrice, the adult Sammy is confronted at the gatehouse by "the stuffed lion and stuffed python and stuffed goat." That he is aware of their moral symbolism is evidenced by his attribution of "the yellow eyes of lust" to the goat. Here, outside the asylum that Sammy knows to be "the house of the pay-off," lurk versions of the three beasts of worldliness that blocked Dante's climb to the Mount of Joy. Dante's lion of violence and ambition is immediately recognizable; his leopard of malice and fraud and she wolf of incontinence reappear in Sammy's python and goat respectively. What makes the parody so hideous is that the three emblematic animals confront Dante at the beginning of the quest, Sammy at the end. Thus the animals at the gatehouse assert that the "house of the pay-off" they guard is not paradise but hell. Waiting to enter the room where Beatrice sits, Sammy accepts the horrid inversion: "Can't you see I am up to the neck in the ice on paradise hill?" In the lowest circle of Dante's *Inferno* is

Satan, fixed in polluted ice. Toward this greatest of all sinners — "the foul creature" who, like Sammy, "once had worn the grace of Paradise" — flow all the rivers of guilt. Within the room where madwomen come and go is Sammy's version of the ninth circle of hell. There Beatrice Ifor survives in a state "rather like...continual and exaggerated worry," a sickening parody of the state of a soul in bliss achieved by Dante's Beatrice.

Free Fall is organized so that Sammy's visit to the madhouse immediately follows his recollection of the moment when he decided to sacrifice everything to possess Beatrice. This cause-and-effect arrangement spotlights Sammy's guilt for Beatrice's degeneration. Although Dr. Enticott offers the consolation that the exact cause of Beatrice's condition cannot be pinpointed, his cryptic review of her medical records — "Heredity. Yes. I see. Illnesses" — actually reinforces the cause-and-effect linkage. At the height — or in the depth — of his desperate pursuit of Beatrice Sammy had once threatened to go mad if she did not yield. Moments before he confronts her in the asylum he recalls her fright: *"You mustn't ever say such a thing, Sammy"* (Golding's italics). It was his feigned madness — an echo of her own putative heredity — that initiated the tragic pattern of cause and effect. Because it was only under the pressure of his threat of madness that Beatrice first yielded, their subsequent love affair, his desertion, and her ultimate reduction to a mindless automaton can fairly be attributed to his fatal deception. A consequence of the decision to seduce Beatrice at all costs, feigned madness marks the boundary between Sammy's innocence and his depravity. The days of innocence embodied in his relationships with Ma and Evie and in his retrospective aphorism — "love selflessly and you cannot come to harm" — are sealed off from the present days of guilt by the barrier erected by his selfishness. And the gravity of his offense is inferred from the prison camp episodes that implicitly compare Sammy's moral crimes to those perpetrated on a far vaster scale by Nazi Germany. Dr. Halde, nearly a caricature of the brutal but sensitive SS officer, plays upon

Sammy's fears much as Sammy had played upon Beatrice's; and in the decline of Halde (*slope* in German) from university professor to SS torturer can be read Sammy's own fall from grace. Both men have chosen to cloak their crimes under the rubric of *rationalism* — a mixed blessing as usual for Golding.

The failure of unalloyed rationalism as a philosophy to live by is recognized by Sammy in the brief chapter that follows him out of the asylum and concludes the novel. At the outset of the chapter Sammy decides to visit his spiritual parents, Nick Shales and Rowena Pringle, avatars of rationalism and religion respectively. To Nick he wants to explain that un-mediated rationalism spawns the male totem (reminiscent of the stag-god in *The Inheritors*) whose modern incarnation is the jackbooted Nazi. But Nick has been reduced by illness to "the image of the labouring mind" and lies "dying of a tired heart." Implied by the atrophic imagery is the exhaustion, even the impossibility, of rationalism as a viable philosophy. What breathed life into Nick's essentially nineteenth-century rationalism (and that of Golding's father) was the inherent morality of its adherents. Lacking their moral stature, mod-ern man (e.g., Sammy) succumbs to his baser nature. A Nick Shales or a Golding père may override or negate the effects of original sin by virtue of his sheer decency; but for the mass of men the wages of godlessness are Sammy's crimes writ large in Nazi atrocities. Thus the inversion of the medieval drama of salvation in *Free Fall*. The only mount of joy to which Sammy Mountjoy has aspired — and the only one he appears to have attained — is not Dante's *Paradiso* but the mons veneris. Still, Miss Pringle is found by Sammy to be liv-ing in a world no less singular and no more complete than Nick's: "She had deceived herself completely." What Sammy predictably concludes is that both worlds are equally real and that the hoped-for bridge between the two does not exist.

This apparently uncertain answer to the problem of belief has led some critics to shift from a moral to an artistic fo-cus. *Free Fall* has therefore been read as a *Künstlerroman* on the order of such classic English novels of artistic maturation as James Joyce's *A Portrait of the Artist as a Young Man* (1916) and D. H. Lawrence's *Sons and Lovers* (1913). Not only is the overtly autobiographical element in such novels present, albeit in muted form, in the aspects of his own life that Golding claims to have reversed in Sammy's. Many other staples of the form are equally evident — the ostensible deprivation but underlying richness of boyhood; the first glimmerings of artistic destiny; the stirrings of sexual desire and the crisis of sexual initiation. Even Golding's symbolic pairings — Johnny Spragg and Philip Arnold; Nick Shales and Rowena Pringle; Dr. Halde and the camp commandant; especially Beatrice and Taffy — invoke the standard oppositions of the *Künstlerroman*. Sammy's initially idealized but ultimately frustrating love of Beatrice — the prelude to and perhaps even the raison d'être for his mundane but fulfilling love of Taffy — mirrors the spirituality of Paul Morel's feeling for Miriam as well as its aftermath in the sensuality of his liaison with Clara in *Sons and Lovers*. Yet despite its occasionally more than superficial affinities with the *Künstlerroman*, *Free Fall* is essentially a novel of a very different order. It is not centrally about Sammy's rise to artistic heights; he is already a famous painter when the novel opens. Rather it is about his fall into the moral depths from which his entire narrative is designed to extricate him by retracing the pattern of events that precipitated it.

That art may be a peripheral issue for Golding becomes clearer when *Free Fall* is read alongside any of the works of the modern master who deals most fully and most powerfully with the artistic persona — Thomas Mann. Already in his monumental first novel, *Buddenbrooks* (1900), Mann gives profound expression to what proves to be his major theme: the conflict between art and life. And in such famous novellas as *Tonio Kröger* (1903) and *Death in Venice* (1911) the conflict is even more sharply focused. Mann's hero-artist, endlessly torn between the mutually exclusive demands of the sensuous and the aesthetic, generally ends by accepting his difference — and his distance — from other men. No comparable seriousness about the artist and his art appears in

Free Fall. While it is true that certain crucial episodes in his life — the affair with Beatrice, the liberation from the prison cell — evoke an artistic response, Sammy thinks of his art as more of a parlor trick than a high calling at those rare moments when he thinks about it at all. The high-powered artist/intellectual, such as Stephen Dedalus in *A Portrait of the Artist as a Young Man* or Adrian Leverkühn, the musical genius of Mann's *Dr. Faustus* (1947), is conspicuously absent from *Free Fall.* Sammy's is a natural talent that has nothing to do with his dismal background or mediocre education. He agonizes no more about its origins than about its products. Never does he preoccupy himself about his identity as artist or about the role of the artist in society, two of the hero's abiding concerns in the *Künstlerroman.*

In fact art has nothing to do with Sammy's fall unless one argues that he is driven to discover the secret of Beatrice's inner being in order to re-create the metaphorical light that he had once captured in a classroom sketch of her. Even if this is momentarily the case, his obsession is soon revealed as sexual rather than aesthetic. Sammy is not the representative modern artist but simply the representative modern man who happens to be an artist. Pincher Martin, Golding's first contemporary adult protagonist, represented man not at his most typical but at his worst. Sammy exists within a social context that creates the sort of explanations for his actions that were largely beside the point in *Pincher Martin,* an eschatological novel that invoked only those brief flashes of quotidian life that were necessary to establish Martin's consummate evil. The quotidian sociology of *Free Fall,* however, is compounded of layers of details that reveal not only Sammy's actions but their antecedents to be more typical than unique. From his childhood infatuation with Evie to his obsession with Beatrice to his fulfillment with Taffy (complete with marriage and child) and even to his illusion of a severed penis, Sammy enacts the drama of post-Freudian man. Not only because sex is his motive force but also because his sexual behavior is so typical, Sammy is Golding's representative modern man. Apropos of

Free Fall, Golding elaborates on an interviewer's point that the love relationship is a "paradigm of the human problem:" "As soon as one partner in this love relationship begins to use the other deliberately and self-consciously and to find a sexual need and satisfaction somehow detached as a separate entity from the total relationship, it's at that moment that the innocence is lost, and one has fallen into a morally diseased relationship."[7]

What would be merely the sexual component of, or a diversion from, artistic development — the critical issue of the *Künstlerroman* — becomes the focal point of the moral inquiry of *Free Fall*. In another sort of novel Sammy might squirm off the moral hook by claiming that as post-Freudian man his actions, including the seduction and desertion of Beatrice, were more typical than aberrant. After all, it is only Beatrice's madness, a condition Sammy could hardly have foreseen, that distinguishes her from the countless deserted lovers who suffer few if any consequences. Dr. Enticott, no friend of Sammy's by the end of their interview, refuses to condemn him outright, acknowledging that the precise cause of Beatrice's insanity cannot be ascertained. And Taffy, as sexually pliable as her name suggests, turns out to be an unexceptionable wife and mother and a partner in an obviously happy marriage.

A slightly cynical reader, conditioned by the sociology and psychology of twentieth-century fiction, might reasonably argue that Beatrice insane differs little from Beatrice in full possession of her faculties. Even her outward beauty was marred by a seemingly invincible blandness and blankness as expressed in her characteristic response to everything: "Maybe." Whatever mystery Sammy sensed and sought behind the exquisite facade of her face seems never to have existed; the radiant Dantean Beatrice was a creature of his imagination. While she cannot be faulted for failing to live up to Sammy's extravagant image of her, by the same token he should not be condemned for seeking sexual fulfillment elsewhere. Yet the argument of *Free Fall* is that there is no moral justification for those who use others for their own selfish ends. Sammy stands indicted not solely or even primarily for Beatrice's life sentence of insanity but for his willingness to do everything to possess her. It is that "everything," in all its frightening implications, that condemns him. Still, he is no monster on the order of a Pincher Martin. In Sammy's ability to feel guilt, in his painful decision to trace it back to its source, and in his refusal to evade responsibility for his actions lies hope of redemption. Given man's inherent depravity for Golding, the fact that Sammy does not hide behind fashionable modern sociological and psychological shibboleths but instead acknowledges the evil at his core is itself potentially redemptive. Although it is true that the "stagnant pool" of Sammy the adult can never regain the pristine clarity of the "spring water" that was Sammy the child, the man who confronts Beatrice in the asylum is in all respects better than the man who betrayed her.

Lest it appear that the unbridgeable gap between flesh and spirit perceived by Sammy after his shattering visit to Beatrice and his inconclusive meetings with Nick Shales and Rowena Pringle constitutes prima facie evidence of an absurd universe, Golding appends his by-now-familiar coda to explode not only the various unitary explanations of existence but equally the explanation that there is no explanation favored by the existentialists. In the return of the commandant to liberate Sammy from the darkness of what was, after all, only a broom closet, and from the fearful guilt that envisioned a severed penis in what was, after all, only a damp rag, Golding plays out to the end the drama of man's contingent existence. The last "inscrutable words" of *Free Fall* are the commandant's: "The Herr Doctor does not know about peoples." Does this cryptic reference invalidate the departed Dr. Halde's conviction about Sammy — as well as all convictions that reduce man to an automaton? Or should the words be read ironically in the light of Sammy's behavior in the "cell" that apparently confirms Halde's view that Sammy possesses "nothing to mark you out from the ants or the sparrows." If Sammy is more than the sum of his appetites, then the confinement in and release from the terror of the cell assumes a pattern of symbolic death and rebirth. While this reverses the plunge into darkness experienced by Pincher Martin, it falls well short of ushering Sammy into a Dantean paradise. The best that can be hoped for him is that by crying out to God and emerging from darkness into light he has arrested his free fall and regained the prospect of redemption. There is, conceivably, beyond what fallible man perceives as cosmic chaos, an ineffable configuration fashioned by God: "It may be — I hope it is — redemption to guess and perhaps perceive that the universe, the hell which we see for all its beauty, vastness, majesty is only part of a whole which is quite unimaginable."[8]

6

God's Visionary: *The Spire*

Not Sammy Mountjoy, the famous painter of *Free Fall,* but Jocelin, Dean of the Cathedral of the Virgin Mary and the protagonist of *The Spire* (1964), is Golding's portrait of the artist. "In so far as, without meaning to, Jocelin has created a work of art, *The Spire* is related to the problem of what is an artist, why is an artist, how is an artist. I would have thought it's more about art than *Free Fall* is."[1] Golding's words make it clear that *The Spire* is vitally concerned with art — its genesis, its form, its execution. And if, like the spire, the work of art owes its inspiration and completion to a single visionary creator, then its identity owes something to his own. This is particularly true when, again like the spire, the finished work of art defies — or transcends — its conceptual and/or material limits. Jocelin, far from a "learned man," much less an architect, envisions the spire not as a pile of stones but as "the ultimate prayer." In his notebook, which he begs Father Adam to read aloud after the spire is erected against all odds, Jocelin had recorded the visionary moment when God inspired him to create "the exact image of my prayer in stone." To an incredulous Roger Mason, the aptly named master builder who flatly tells him that the cathedral foundations cannot support a four-hundred-foot spire, Jocelin replies that it is divinely ordained: "God revealed it to me in a vision." According to Jocelin, what God chose him to envision He chooses Mason "to fill...with glass and iron and stone" so that "our spire will be a diagram of the highest prayer of all." In his monomaniacal devotion to building the spire, Jocelin emulates the blind faith that inspired the equally problematic construction of Salisbury Cathedral, as recounted by Golding:

Round about the year 1200, Bishop Poore was standing on a hill overlooking the confluence of the local rivers, according to legend, when the mother of Jesus appeared to him, told him to shoot an arrow and build her a church where the arrow fell. The arrow flew more than a mile and fell in the middle of a swamp. There, with complete indifference to such things as health, foundations, access and general practicability, the cathedral was built. Eighty years later, with a technological gamble which makes space travel seem child's play, the builders erected the highest spire in the country on top of it, thousands of tons of lead and iron and wood and stone. Yet the whole building still stands. It leans. It totters. It bends. But it still stands... a perpetual delight, a perpetual wonder.[2]

That Jocelin's cathedral shares with its original a marshy site and an outsize spire is less important than their common birth in mystical experience. For about twenty years Golding taught school with the spire of Salisbury Cathedral "sticking up outside the window," constantly amazed that "it should be there... and that someone should have done it."[3] To "invent the circumstances... and the sort of person" behind its erection is ultimately to conduct not primarily a historical or even an aesthetic but rather a moral inquiry along familiar Golding lines. *Barchester Spire,* the novel's original title, became *The Spire* because Golding abandoned his "idea of writing some Barchester-like novel." No one of Trollope's many Barchester novels that so exhaustively chronicle the social milieu of Golding's environs is invoked or inverted in *The Spire,* whose altered title reveals Golding's generic rather than Trollope's local intentions. So determined was Golding to write about what Trollope so strangely ignored — the cathedral and its "preposterous" spire — that he "deliberately knocked a couple of transepts off" the real Salisbury Cathedral.[4] The playful disclaimer of historicity reflects Golding's insistence that, resemblances to Salisbury Cathedral notwithstanding, "the Spire could have been anywhere. I was writing about a cathedral of the mind."[5]

The mind that conceived the cathedral spire on the strength of a miraculous vision belongs to a man dedicated to fulfilling at all costs what he takes to be God's will. At first Jocelin reckons the cost in money; but even when he begins to understand that there will be human costs as well he never wavers. The human factor is first apparent in the estrangement from his old friend and confessor, Father Anselm. Jocelin's subsequent decision to change confessors seems unremarkable; but since he ends by having no confessor at all, it constitutes an early symptom of spiritual deflection. This symbolic standstill in his own spiritual life is reflected in his disruption of the general spiritual life of the cathedral. Priests and congregants alike are diverted from their routines of worship by Mason's "army" of workers who all but take over the cathedral. And because the workers are mostly pagans, their very presence is an affront to the faithful, nearly all of whom were opposed to the spire in the first place. The general fears are echoed by Pangall (Pang/all) whose cottage abutting the cathedral is overwhelmed by building materials and who predicts that the savage workers, having already killed one man, will one day kill him. Despite Jocelin's assurances to the contrary, Pangall will eventually fall victim to the army. The failure to prevent Pangall's murder is a far graver instance of the neglect that causes Jocelin to forgo confession. And Pangall's is but one of the many lives that will be sacrificed to the spire. Well before Pangall's murder, the falling-out with Anselm had already evoked the more than monetary costs of spire building. While the rupture between them grieves Jocelin, it actually strengthens his resolve: "I didn't know how much you would cost up there, the four hundred feet of you. I thought you would cost no more than money. But still, cost what you like."

A surefire recipe for evil in Golding's moral calculus, Jocelin's "cost what you like" hauntingly recalls Sammy Mountjoy's sacrifice of "everything" to possess Beatrice in *Free Fall*. The tragic consequences of single-minded obsession are as unforeseen by Jocelin as they were by Sammy. Again, what is so damning is not the obsession per se but its pursuit at all costs. Unlike Sammy, whose motives are purely — and admittedly — self serving, Jocelin claims higher than personal justification. "It's God's will in this business," he replies to Mason's assertion that the cathedral's foundation cannot support the weight of the spire. It is precisely this oft-repeated rationale that most clearly reflects Jocelin's sin. From his endless juxtapositions of God's will and his own it is evident that he equates the two. Belying his self-characterization as the humble instrument of God's will, however, is the manner in which he asserts his own will against others. As arrogant as he is self-righteous, Jocelin reduces his fellow human beings to building material. Alison's money, Anselm's friendship, Mason's sanity, and the lives of the Pangalls are sacrificed to the spire. Nowhere is Jocelin's playing God more obvious or insidious than in his dealings with Roger Mason who sporadically threatens to stop work on a project he regards as both dangerous and foolhardy. By ruthlessly cutting off all possibilities of work elsewhere for Mason and his army, and particularly by hypocritically closing his eyes to the builder's affair with Goody Pangall — "She will keep him here" — Jocelin bends Mason to his will. At the height — or in the depths — of his power over Mason, Jocelin exultingly identifies his own aims with God's: "And this is how a will feels when it is linked to a Will without limit or end." Another example of the devastating consequences of playing God immediately follows Jocelin's subjugation of Mason. As if to bear out the builder's dire predictions, stones crumble, the earth trembles, and Pangall is killed by the terrified rioting workers.

In his overweening pride Jocelin recalls certain heroes of Greek and Shakespearean tragedy. Like Sophocles' Oedipus who, having solved the riddle of the Sphinx, deems himself infallible, Jocelin rejects all versions of reality but his own. Oedipus's browbeating of Tiresias and his refusal to credit the wisdom of the blind seer corresponds to Jocelin's treatment of Roger Mason. Like *Oedipus the King, The Spire* records the dire consequences of pride: Jocelin's leads directly to the manipulating of people, to the neglect of priestly duties, to the desecration of the cathedral, to the countenancing of adultery and murder, and somewhat less directly to the deaths of the Pangalls and to the destruction of Mason. Most striking, and most damning, of all is Jocelin's certainty that he, like Oedipus, possesses knowledge so privileged as to be more divine than human. The human cost of erecting the spire approaches the devastation wreaked on friend and foe alike by Shakespeare's King Lear. Lear's decision to divide his kingdom and his equally irresponsible manipulating of his daughters in so doing is replicated in Jocelin's similarly irrevocable decision to build the spire and to sacrifice everyone and everything else to its completion. The many calamities spawned by pride in *Oedipus the King, King Lear,* and *The Spire* are incarnated in crime-and-punishment scenarios that are themselves reflections of the religious sensibilities of their authors. That pride goeth before a fall is demonstrated in each case by the damage the protagonist inflicts upon himself and others in the course of playing God. And in each case it is possible that the unforeseen tragedies resulting from hubris constitute divine retribution for a blasphemous masquerade.

In his confidence of God's favor Jocelin is, like Oedipus, guilty of the sin of presumption. Because the dean is a medieval churchman his brand of hubris assumes Christian coloration. Thus he imagines himself a saint visited periodically by a guardian angel whose warm breath on his back is a palpable sign of God's grace. In casting the angel as God's messenger, sent "to comfort me. As it was of old, in the desert," Jocelin dares even to cast himself as Christ. That his blasphemy is unconscious and his self-image curiously innocent are reflected in his cry to God immediately after one of his angelic visitations: *"Lord, I thank Thee that Thou hast kept me humble!"* This unintentionally ironic note of humility is struck again in chapter 4 when Jocelin, persisting in his imitation of Christ, repeats "I am about my Father's business." Coming at a time when, oblivious to his flock and forgetful of the sacraments, he has all but ceased to function as a priest, Jocelin's identification with Christ is glaringly sinful. As it mounts ever higher the spire becomes the outward semblance of Jocelin's soaring pride. Soaring imagery is explicitly invoked in Jocelin's resemblance to an eagle, the bird of pride. Carved in stone by the dumb sculptor, Jocelin's profile features a nose "like an eagle's beak," its "nostrils strained wide...like a pair of wings the wide, blind eyes." The stone likeness captures hubris in action, straining blindly. Intended to pierce the sky at a height previously unimagined, the spire recalls the biblical Tower of Babel whose builders aspired to scale the heights of heaven. The self-aggrandizement that inspired the tower is evoked in Jocelin's wish that the spire could be "a thousand feet high" so that he might "oversee the whole country." As the spire nears completion, Jocelin more and more compulsively climbs to its top where one day he spots his reflection in a metal sheet. More than ever the nose is "like a beak and now nearly as sharp." As the spire rises in tandem with his vision, Jocelin's already strong identification with the eagle of pride grows even stronger. Sighting a "great bird" in the air and "remembering Saint John," Jocelin neatly dovetails associations. His mistaken assertion that the bird is an eagle, the emblem of Saint John the Divine, is particularly revealing. When corrected, Jocelin insists: "Well. As far as I am concerned it is an eagle." So reflexive and persistent is his identification with the eagle and the saint — and the visionary power they share — that he refashions reality to perpetuate his self-image.

As the spire ascends heavenward Jocelin increasingly associates it with himself. This personal, even proprietary, view of the spire risks subverting its raison d'être. The spire of Jocelin's mystical vision was supposed to be a visible expression of faith, a prayer translated into stone as a monument to God. Yet even as he multiplies his references to the holy genesis, nature, and function of the spire, Jocelin's invocations of God increasingly, if subconsciously, valorize himself. The proprietary attitude toward the spire reflected in his juxtapositions of God's will and his own until the two become indistinguishable symptomizes Jocelin's general outlook. "My place, my house, my people," he exclaims, looking around the cathedral he has put on "like a coat." During the early stages of construction he imagines himself a surgeon taking a knife to the stomach of "my church." So absolutely does Jocelin identify with the cathedral that its "body" becomes his own. He compares the old model of the cathedral with its newly affixed spire — his "diagram of prayer" — to "a man lying on his back." Other people are similarly regarded as extensions of himself rather than as valuable in themselves. Tools to be manipulated in a self-aggrandizing project, the Masons, the Pangalls, Fathers Anselm and Adam, Lady Alison are patronized, employed, or dismissed as the situation seems to warrant. To Jocelin, Mason, for example, is no more than his "slave for the work." With his every success in reducing people to bit players in his master plot, Jocelin opens a breach between himself and his fellowmen. Beginning as early as the time when he ran roughshod over those members of his chapter who opposed the spire, and recurring in the frequent clashes with Roger Mason that constitute much of the novel's drama, Jocelin's refusal to tolerate dissent epitomizes his pride as it exacerbates his alienation.

Throughout the first half of *The Spire* Jocelin's appropriation of the cathedral, of human beings, even of the will of God, describes the rising arc of the tragic hero's fortunes. Like Oedipus's and Lear's, Jocelin's is essentially a drama of self-assertion. The four images of his head carved in stone "shall be built in, two hundred feet up, on every side of the tower, mouth open, proclaiming day and night till doomsday." By embedding his likeness in the four corners of the spire Jocelin has made God's house his own. Indeed the dean's self-immortalizing "doomsday" casts himself as more nearly the equal rather than the servant of God. And the spire, in its conception a monument to God's glory, becomes in its execution a monument to Jocelin's pride. This habit of self-aggrandizement, censurable in an Oedipus or a Lear, should be anathema to a medieval churchman who professes the doctrine of *contemptus mundi*. Because the doctrine disdains this world in favor of heaven, self-effacement rather than self-assertion should ideally characterize human behavior. A worldview that sees in salvation the only reward cannot fail to regard worldly ambition as futile when not actually counterproductive. That man is born but to die is the formula of Gothic tragedy: the higher the heights to which the protagonist rises, the more precipitous must be his fall. It is the finitude of human existence that Jocelin as dean of a cathedral should impress upon his followers by urging them to forsake earthly ambition rather than by advancing his own. But his pride so estranges him from his flock and from his priestly duties as to drive him to enact the very tragedy it is his vocation to prevent. Nowhere is Jocelin's pastoral estrangement more glaringly apparent than during his critical confrontation with Roger Mason that ends with the builder's being forced to go on with the spire. In Jocelin's eyes the reluctant Mason is no more than an "animal" to be trapped. That all are diminished in Jocelin's sight is evidenced in his explicit disavowal of the priest's primary mission — the saving of souls: "But we are each responsible for our own salvation." It is as much for his diminishment of others as for his exaltation of himself that Jocelin stands indicted for the sin of pride.

If the rising spire represents Jocelin's estrangement from his fellowmen it also indicates his likeness to them. This dual symbolism is already apparent at the outset of the novel when Jocelin compares the cathedral model to a "man lying on his back." The wooden spire — "springing, projecting, bursting, erupting" from the model into which he has "jammed it" — incarnates Jocelin's phallic as well as his spiritual aspirations. Golding's half-serious proposal to call the novel *An Erection at Barchester* highlights the centrality of its hero's sexual motivation. As in *Pincher Martin* and *Free Fall*, male sexuality expresses itself in egocentric assertion. Sexual aggressiveness, overt in Martin and Mountjoy and thus directed toward women, is in Jocelin necessarily repressed and thus deflected toward the spire. What Golding demonstrates in

The Spire is that sexual obsession may serve as a metaphor for human sinfulness in a celibate priest as well as in itchy post-Freudian youths. The spire — "an implacable, unstoppable, glorious fountain of the spirit, a wild burning of me for Thee" — that Jocelin records in his notebook is as sexual as it is spiritual. Typically ambiguous in its "Thee," Jocelin's emotional ecstasy reflects his long-repressed lust for the red-haired Goody Pangall as much as his love for God. This ambiguity persists until the very end of *The Spire* where the dying Jocelin's last gasp "might be interpreted as a cry of *God! God! God!*" — or perhaps *Goody! Goody! Goody!* In the workers' riot that immediately follows Roger Mason's forecast of disaster, the underlying sexual imagery of the first half of *The Spire* surfaces most explicitly. Jocelin sees the model of the spire projecting "obscenely" from between the legs of one of Pangall's murderers; at the same time he glimpses Goody, her hair a "cloud of red" and her belly shining "through the hand-torn gap in her dress," staring across the pit at Mason as though confirming their illicit affair. The converging sexual imagery spotlights Jocelin's repressed desires and their moral consequences. Yearning for Goody he had symbolically preserved her for himself by marrying her to the impotent Pangall and then sacrificed her anew to Mason in order to keep the builder working on the spire. As the events of the riot scene make clear, Jocelin bears primary responsibility for the fate of the three people he has thus manipulated.

Of the several tragedies sparked by the volatile combination of Jocelin's spiritual and phallic aspirations, Goody's is most crucial to the overarching design of *The Spire*. Jocelin's repressed longing for Goody dehumanizes her in much the same fashion as Sammy Mountjoy's passion reduces Beatrice to a sexual object in *Free Fall*. A cardinal sin for Golding, the violation of the total personality by isolating its sexual component diminishes violated and violator alike. Jocelin is haunted by Goody's red hair, the erotic emblem to which he has reduced her. As nothing but a shock of red hair, Goody serves his sexual needs, just as Mason, as nothing but a trapped animal, serves his building needs. So completely does her blazing hair fill his thoughts, both waking and sleeping, that it becomes his primary mode of perception. At those times when he is most aware of her sexual nature, the red hair is omnipresent. Immediately after discovering Goody with Roger Mason ("She will keep him here") Jocelin jams the spire "into the square hole" of the cathedral model as it "lay on its back." This sexual gesture prefigures a dream that night in which he is visited by Satan "clad in nothing but blazing hair." The merger of Satan and Goody triggers ejaculation; and Jocelin awakens so full of self-loathing that he flagellates himself. After Goody exchanges glances with Mason during the workers' riot, Jocelin tries to "re-create the peaceful woman behind the hair." But the hair, once sprung from the "decent covering of the wimple," cannot be put back again. Trying to recall the innocent Goody, Jocelin finds that the red hair has "erased" the past. No longer able to envision the whole woman, he finds himself "looking" at the red hair instead.

Although the masturbatory fantasy of Satan clothed in blazing hair conflates Jocelin's repressed lust for Goody and the guilt it engenders, it is in her death scene that the red hair imagery is most fully orchestrated. Outside Pangall's cottage, clutching the money Stilbury demands to accept the pregnant Goody, Jocelin encounters Rachel Mason, "a wisp of red hair caught in her fingers." Inside the cottage Goody cringes before the fire, "a cascade of red, torn hair" falling from her head. As Jocelin's "long shadow" falls across her, she screams — "I was the accuser and she fled from me," he later acknowledges — and goes on screaming as she "grabbed her belly with both hands." Then "there was blood over the money on the floor"; and when Jocelin stumbles out of the cottage and into the choir to pray for Goody, "the hair and the blood blinded the eyes of his mind." This commingling of Goody's hair and blood — the respective symbols of Jocelin's sin and its awful wages — triggers an agonizing and long-overdue self-reappraisal. That her blood is on his hands is evoked in the grisly image of the bloodstained money, the very money he would use to send her away. Figuratively as well as literally blood money, it is emblematic of Jocelin's moral stain. An inkling of his own part in shielding himself from reality may be evinced in Jocelin's "I was a protected man." Hair and blood combine again, surging into his consciousness to expose his former actions toward Goody for the series of manipulations they actually were. At the climax of his self-indicting epiphany, just prior to learning of Goody's death, Jocelin achieves full awareness of the "totality of his life, his sins, and his forced cruelty, and above all the dreadful glow of his dedicated will." This moment of self-recognition — "like a birth itself" — an indispensable stage in the evolution of the tragic hero, is crystallized in the words of an Easter song: *"This have I done for my true love."* Like corresponding recognition epiphanies in the Greek and Shakespearean drama that Golding so much admires, Jocelin's resonates with an irony as devastating as it is all-revealing.

Goody's affective power lives on after her death. Haunted by her "white body and irretrievable blood," Jocelin inches toward the humility he had all along professed in theory but denied in practice: "I'm not very intelligent." Yet the after-effects of his culpability linger on in his recurring vision of her white body and red blood that results in "the present impossibility of prayer." Unable to banish the dead Goody or to ignore the changes in Roger Mason who, symbolically enchained by his wife, has taken to drink and has come to resemble a trapped animal, Jocelin more and more compulsively seeks refuge from his tutelary demons atop the spire. Only in the increasingly rarefied atmosphere of the ascending spire can he maintain a vestige of his once absolute identification of God's will with his own. At ground level, endlessly afflicted by the remembrance of "certain things that had happened to him," Jocelin cries out in the past tense: *"There was God!"* Increasingly he identifies with the laborers, working alongside them on the spire that alone "put the thoughts out of his head." Just as he had once overlooked murder and condoned adultery, Jocelin now ignores the workers' paganism.

That he has not fully comprehended the lesson of Goody's death and Mason's decline is evident in his conviction that the pagan workers are "good men" who "were chosen just as I was chosen." Like the Pangalls and the Masons, Jocelin's four human pillars at the crossways of the cathedral, the workers are essentially building material. And just as his self-justifying ego refashions their lives according to his needs, it transforms the pagan workers into God's chosen. Again, however, Jocelin is forced by circumstance to confront the truth, this time when his "crew of good men" joins "the devil worshippers out on the hills" in a Midsummer Night ritual. And again his reluctant knowledge is achieved in images of fire and blood. As Jocelin recalls the guilt of David, who "could not build the temple because he had blood on his hands," the "vast fire" of the pagan rite turns into "all the fires of hell" amidst which a spectral Goody materializes at his side. Knowing now that the workers are devil worshippers and therefore that the "obscene" mistletoe berry he spotted during their riot is a sacrificial token, Jocelin is staggered by the realization that Pangall was ritually murdered. Whether this truth is indeed an epiphanic revelation, or like the shock of recognition that revealed his yearning for Goody, merely the surfacing of long-repressed knowledge, its effect is to remind Jocelin yet again of the human cost of the spire.

The hellfire and brimstone imagery of his Midsummer Night epiphany instills in Jocelin the same terror that overcame him when the rioting workers murdered Pangall. Dramatized in both scenes is the "lesson for this height" that accompanies each stage of the spire's erection. Gradually, the rising spire — the projection of Jocelin's mounting pride — comes also to represent his incremental attainment of knowledge. Like Greek and Shakespearean tragedy *The Spire* incorporates the education of a protagonist into the life of its design. Although the novel can be said to consist broadly of two movements — the building of the spire (chapters 1–9) and the final reckoning of its cost (chapters 10–12) — the course of Jocelin's development suggests a triadic structure. Each of the three roughly equal "acts" culminates in a visionary recognition scene: the workers' riot (chapter 4); the Midsummer Night devil worship (chapter 8); the deathbed revelation (chapter 12). To ripen in knowledge Jocelin must, like Oedipus and Lear, be totally stripped of his illusions. Those that remain after Midsummer Night are swiftly dispelled in the last "act" of *The Spire*. Jocelin learns not only that the spire was financed chiefly by the tainted money of his aunt but that his deanship was procured by her sexual services to the former king. Then comes the dumb carver's ironic revelation that the apparently solid cathedral pillars Jocelin had trusted to support the spire consist merely of "stone skin" filled with rubble. As Faith, Jocelin had always countered Mason's Reason with belief in miracle, belief that gained credibility when the cathedral itself was found to be built on mud. Yet both men had assumed that the pillars were solid. Jocelin's "miracle" was based on stone; that of the "giants," who built on mud and filled pillars with rubble, on real faith. Chastened in spirit by this latest proof of his own shortcomings, Jocelin now suffers the terrible physical chastisement administered by the angel at his back. His punishment, a vastly harsher version of the self-flagellation that followed his masturbatory dream, serves also to clarify the meaning of the warm breath on his back. What Jocelin in his pride took for God's ministering angel is actually the spinal tuberculosis that will shortly kill him. In the angel's duality the connection between the spirit and the flesh that Jocelin denied is explicitly revealed. Now he imagines his former guardian angel to be the "dark angel," a tormenting devil sent to plague rather than to comfort him. Still, he clings to the consoling fiction that flesh has been sacrificed to spirit. That vestiges of his pride linger on is evident in Jocelin's reference to the spire as "*my* prayer." As though to rebuke him for persisting in identifying his will with God's, the dark angel instantly fells him with another devastating blow. Although the repeated attacks also signal his impending death, enough time remains for Jocelin to gain further insight. In dragging his wasted body from his sickbed down to the village to ask

Roger Mason's forgiveness, Jocelin finally breaks his habit of rejecting the human for the divine. This symbolic as well as actual descent from the cathedral close to the village gutter is punctuated by flashing glimpses of the apple tree and king-fisher that will reappear to him in a deathbed vision. Mason, by now a hopeless drunkard and potential suicide, can nei-ther fathom nor assuage Jocelin's guilt. Yet in submitting to the judgment of his fellow man by facing Mason "in pain and shame" to beg his forgiveness Jocelin achieves genuine hu-mility. And in removing his skullcap, laying aside his cross, even apologizing for his tonsure, Jocelin, not as priest but simply as man, stands before Mason in recognition of their common humanity. Stripped like Oedipus and Lear of the ac-cidents of rank, Jocelin is similarly revealed as the "poor, bare, fork'd animal" that Shakespeare's fallen king calls "unaccom-modated man." As neither more nor less than a man — whose "stink" does Mason "good" — Jocelin sums up the lesson he has learned: "To love all men with a holy love." It is the lesson learned in *Free Fall* by Sammy Mountjoy who emerged from a prison cell to locate his "vital morality" in "the relationship of individual man to individual man."

That Jocelin no longer denies the full implications of his humanity is apparent in his recourse to the pit imagery that throughout *The Spire* has suggested the dark region of man's mind. The "stink" that Mason attributes to Jocelin (and that Lear smells on himself) ironically recalls the place "where the pit stinks" and where Jocelin first received his vision of the spire. While he had condemned the "filthy" pit in others, he had denied its existence in himself. In revealing to Mason — and acknowledging to himself — the dark wellsprings of mo-tivation that brought about so much human tragedy, notably Goody's, Jocelin achieves the self-knowledge requisite for re-demption. His many references to the "cellarage" of the mind as well as his self-characterization — "I'm a building with a vast cellarage where rats live" — recall the cellar imagery of *Pincher Martin*. Unlike Martin, however, Jocelin is not evil, only errant. That his humanity is not missing, only obscured, is shown by contrast with the unforgiving Father Anselm who coldly rebuffs Jocelin's attempt to patch up their friendship. Jocelin's guilt derives not so much from contempt for people as from subordinating them to the demands of his vision. He atones not only in his confession but in its aftermath when, set upon in a "dark alley," he cries out to his attackers, "My children! My children!" Thus accepting in love the hate of the people he had sinned against in neglect, Jocelin also accepts the scapegoat role he had conferred upon Pangall. In symbolic retribution for sacrificing Pangall to the spire, he sacrifices himself to the mob. Self-sacrifice, hitherto expressed in Jocelin's apparently self-serving spine for spire formula, gains new meaning in the blows he willingly endures and in the echo of Christ in "My children! My children." Authentic where once it would have been ironic, the identification with Christ announces a new Jocelin, purged like Oedipus and Lear of his ego and thus empowered to achieve through suffering the tragic hero's full awareness.

If *The Spire* were Greek or Shakespearian tragedy it might culminate in the village with Jocelin's successive epiphanies of human solidarity. He has descended to the village, however, not solely on a mission of atonement but also in an attempt to solve the mystery of the spire. For the ultimate meaning of the novel is suggested no less by its title than by its protagonist. In this light, Jocelin's meeting with Roger Mason is the symbolic reunification of the vision and the execution that went into the spire. As a reminder of the necessary interdependence of visionary eye and executing hand their meeting may also resolve the dualism of spirit and flesh. Yet this critical symbiosis may account for the spire's completion but not for its endurance in defiance of the laws of gravity. Retrieved from the village gutter and restored to the sickbed that will shortly be his deathbed, the half-delirious Jocelin asks of Father Adam a single question: "Fallen?" The question, like the equally cryptic answer — "Not yet" — refers ostensibly to the spire yet tangentially to Jocelin. Question and answer implicitly link the viability of the work of art with the spiritual status of its creator. Musing along similar lines in "Among School Children" W. B. Yeats asks, "How can we know the dancer from the dance?" To Father Adam, a moral accountant, the issue is eschatological: the not-yet-fallen Jocelin may still be helped into heaven. Even translated into eschatological terms question and answer retain their ambiguity. Given that all men are products of the fall, it follows that all of their works reflect the imperfections of the human condition. What strikes Golding about Salisbury Cathedral is equally true of Jocelin's spire and of mankind: "It leans. It totters. It bends. But it still stands."

Golding's trademark coda is no mere gimmick in *The Spire*. Had the novel ended in the village, the probability of Jocelin's redemption could be extrapolated from his imitation of Christ. But key questions concerning the relationship of the artist to the work of art would have gone unanswered. It is the function of the deathbed scene to clarify that relationship and in so doing, to assess the meaning of a life whose value cannot be determined apart from its single transcendent purpose.

When the dying Jocelin learns of Mason's suicide attempt and that the once-dynamic builder is now blind and dumb, a burnt-out case "beyond communication," this latest evidence of the human cost of the spire edges him toward despair. "If I could go back," thinks Jocelin, "I would take God as lying between people and to be found there." Because he cannot go back and undo the effects of seeking God in the wrong places, Jocelin can do little but reject the visionary mysticism that led him into error. This now causes him to err in the opposite direction: the "cellarage" expands from a part to the whole of the human mind. A vision of "a tangle of hair, blazing among the stars; and the great club of the spire lifted towards it" convinces Jocelin that what he took for divine inspiration was "witchcraft" and that the spire is no more than a monument to his repressed sexuality. That he "traded a stone hammer for four people" Jocelin now takes as proof of his unworthiness and even of his unfitness for heaven. So alienated is he from his former vision that he no longer senses God's presence in the spire: "There is no innocent work. God knows where God may be."

Jocelin's despair is as extravagant as his former euphoria. According to his either-or moral calculus, if he is not inspired by God then he must be deceived by witchcraft. Until the final moments of his life it never occurs to Jocelin that he — and the spire — are amalgams of both the spiritual and the sensual. To define man and his works in exclusive terms is to deny the reality of their makeup. The as yet unreconciled components of the human condition appear before Jocelin as "two eyes looking at him through the panic" of approaching death. But his descent into the village, his confrontation with Roger Mason, and most of all, his surrender to the mob, have won for Jocelin the full humanity that at the point of death empowers him to reconcile spirit and flesh, good and evil, innocence and guilt. "The two eyes slid together" and reveal themselves as the window through which Jocelin for the first and last time sees the completed spire, "slim as a girl," reaching "to infinity in cascades of exultation that nothing could trammel." His reaction to this luminous vision is at once humble and deeply affirmative: "Now — I know nothing at all." Like Oedipus and Lear, Jocelin achieves tragic stature in trading assertion for acceptance. To know nothing, to appreciate the limits of human perception, is, in a sense, to know everything. Jocelin's final vision of the spire — *It's like the apple tree!"* — transforms a dichotomous image into a unified symbol of the artist and the work of art. For the apple tree, like the spire and the man who conceived it, is bound to earth but bent on heaven.

The miracle of a spire that bends but does not fall is Jocelin's vindication and his salvation. Built on human sacrifice but also on human faith, the spire is emblematic of man's dual nature — a distended phallus but also "a diagram of prayer." Jocelin, who nailed the spire to the sky, was, after all, chosen by God. Asked by an interviewer whether Jocelin's conclusion — "There is no innocent work. God knows where God may be" — means that God is driven out of cathedrals by the

evident egoism, fanaticism, and corruption of their builders,
Golding replied:

I would hope that God is merciful. Unless human beings build a
cathedral nobody's going to, and so the cathedral has to be what
humans make of it. To that extent, yes, building always is corrupt
because people always are to some extent corrupt. I don't find God
driven out in that way. It's the best we can do, and I would find Him
beckoned in.[6]

Between the Acts:
The Pyramid and *The Scorpion God:*
Three Short Novels

"Men are prisoners of their metaphors," concludes Golding in "Egypt from My Outside," a 1977 essay inspired by the fulfillment of his long-cherished dream of visiting Egypt.[1] Chief among the Egyptian metaphors that had haunted him from childhood is the pyramid: "For sixty years I had felt how awful yet how necessary it would be to enter the Great Pyramid."[2] The title, the epigraph, and the symbolism of *The Pyramid* (1967); and the setting and the society of the title story of *The Scorpion God: Three Short Novels* (1971) reflect Golding's lifelong obsession with Egypt and its most evocative symbol. In these works Golding's Egyptology, which had surfaced in Sammy Mountjoy's fascination with pictures of Egyptian kings in *Free Fall* and in the medievalized pyramid of *The Spire,* finds its fullest expression. Both *The Pyramid* and *The Scorpion God* collect three stories, and both contain previously published material. The first and third sections of *The Pyramid* appeared a year before the publication of the entire work; "Envoy Extraordinary," the concluding tale of *The Scorpion God,* dates from 1956 when it was published in a volume called *Sometime Never* along with two stories by other writers. Although all three stories in *The Scorpion God* are anthropological fables that take an essentially comic view of history, what unity the book possesses "was not intentional," according to Golding. Wanting to preserve "Envoy

Extraordinary" and needing "a story to go with it … I wrote
'The Scorpion God.' Then I wrote 'Clonk, Clonk' to keep the
other two stories apart, and also make it a book."[3]

The Pyramid

Given the prior — and separate — publication of two of the
three sections of *The Pyramid*, its unity would seem to be
as suspect as that of *The Scorpion God*. True, the triadic
structure of *The Pyramid* conforms to the geometry of the
title: three people who played key roles in the life of the
narrator, Oliver, are recalled in three discrete but necessarily overlapping episodes. And the single setting (Stilbourne
Village), point of view (Oliver's), and theme (initiation) lend
cohesiveness to Golding's most episodic work to date. Yet for
Golding the unity of *The Pyramid* is neither accidental nor
artificial but intentional and real: "It is sonata form really, it's
musical. With a scherzo in the middle … and then it finishes
with a Beethoven set of variations." As a three-movement
composition the sonata recapitulates and embellishes the triadic structural metaphor of the title. Moreover, the sonata
relates intimately to Oliver: "If he had any passion it was for
music, but because of society he ends up making poison gas."[4]
By opposing music to poison gas Golding makes it clear that
the sonata form reflects the morality no less than the structure
of *The Pyramid*. So insistent is he on its structural integrity
in general and on its musical analogy in particular that he
bristles at an interviewer's reference to the "three episodes"
of *The Pyramid*: "Three movements," Golding amends.[5]

All three movements of the novel, set in the appropriately
named Stilbourne village and related by a first-person narrator
known only as Oliver, are constituted primarily as initiation
experiences. Two take place in the 1930s, the first immediately
before and the second a few years after Oliver matriculates at
Oxford. In the final movement it is 1963, and Oliver's perspective is no longer that of callow youth but of settled middle age.

Always there is music. Oliver begins his narration just after playing Chopin's C-Minor Study on the piano; he plays the violin in the amateur theatrical featured in the novel's second movement; and finally, before the grave of his former music teacher, Miss Dawlish, the now middle-aged businessman reinterprets the past by remembering long-ago music lessons. In the course of *The Pyramid* the ambiguity of the music symbolism deepens even as music itself recedes from Oliver's life. Music is initially an entirely positive signifier: Oliver's puppy love for Imogen may be puerile, but its expression on the piano is heartfelt. In the central section of *The Pyramid* Oliver gets over his senseless crush; but he never replaces it with an emotion any more passionate or honest than the one he poured out playing Chopin. Although the Oxford-bound Oliver has already opted for the safety of science over the riskiness of art, music rather than chemistry seems truly to engage him. And music retains its positive attributes especially in light of his wartime activity of making poison gas, a by-product of his career choice.

Yet even at its most positive music can do no more in *The Pyramid* than suggest what might have been. More often it is perverted in the service of attitudes that belie its conventionally positive literary function. In *The Pyramid* these attitudes reflect the intense class consciousness of nearly everyone in Stilbourne, a village whose name epitomizes the moribundity of a class-ridden society. Those associated most closely with music embody not the passion and freedom of the Chopin Oliver plays so compulsively during his last summer before Oxford but the rigidity and conformity of provincial life at its most banal. Oliver's reticent and repressed father and snobbish and smug mother are relentlessly musical; and his own musicality is similarly compromised by its social context. Thus he and his parents align music with their middle-class status. Oliver sneers at Evie's predilection for pop music as a badge of social inferiority; when it turns out that she sings beautifully, in apparent violation of her class origins, he is nonplussed. Music becomes a weapon during the production of the Stilbourne Operatic Society when Oliver's strident violin playing steals a key scene from Norman Claymore, the smarmy male lead. Oliver's triumph and Claymore's upstaging are greeted with delight by Oliver's mother "at the piano, nodding her head and applauding." Music has discomfited the detested Claymore, whose superior social standing and patronizing air gall Oliver's mother. Significantly, and ironically, these two class-conscious snobs have just squared off against each other in a silly squabble that reflects the typical pettiness of their social instincts. Claymore, nearly apoplectic at Oliver's mother's suggestion that her son be addressed as "General" on stage, finally, and only with the utmost reluctance, agrees to call him "Captain." Of the many subversions of music in *The Pyramid* none is more striking than Miss Dawlish's epitaph: "Heaven is Music." Stilbourne — and Oliver — had assumed that the spinster teacher's outwardly barren life was enriched and even redeemed by her apparent dedication to music. When Oliver discovers the charred remains of her sheet music and metronome and the smashed bust of Beethoven in the dead woman's garden, the sad truth about Miss Dawlish is revealed. Far from a heaven, her life in music was actually a hell.

Like Oliver and his parents and nearly everyone else in Stilbourne, Miss Dawlish is class-ridden. Although *The Pyramid* shares the general geographical setting of its immediate predecessor, it is as English as *The Spire* is universal. So localized is *The Pyramid* that several of its characters are named after actual places on the Devon coast such as Dawlish and Babbacombe. Because it is so very English it is occasionally difficult for readers unfamiliar with its geographical and social landscapes to understand. Yet its intense Englishness is indispensable to its central theme — the corrosive influence of a provincial society very like the one in which Golding grew up: "In the dreadful English scheme of things at that time, a scheme which so accepted social snobbery as to elevate it to an instinct, we had our subtle place. . . . In fact, like everybody except the very high and the very low in those days, we walked a social tightrope."[6] In an interview shortly after the 1980 publication of *Rites of Passage,* another very English novel, Golding's hatred of that scheme is palpable: "It was about as stratified a society as you could find anywhere in the country, and I think that the pyramidical structure of English society is present, and my awareness of it is indelibly imprinted in me, in my psyche, not merely in my intellect but very much in my emotional, almost my physical being. I am enraged by it and I am unable to escape it entirely.... It dissolves but it doesn't disappear; it's fossilized in me."[7] Fatally conditioned by the "pyramidical structure" of a society identical to that of Golding's childhood, Stilbourne people rigidify in their social roles. Although love and music figure prominently in *The Pyramid,* both are subsumed under the dominant rubric of the novel: class. The determinism of its central metaphor is nicely illustrated by the foreshortened and exaggeratedly pyramidical metronome, fire licking at its base, that dominates the cover of the American paperback edition of *The Pyramid* (Harcourt Brace Jovanovich, 1967).

If the pyramid as metronome expresses the motif of music, then its three sides express the motif of love. All three movements of *The Pyramid* dramatize the failure of love on the part of characters who play greater (Evie in the first, Miss Dawlish in the third) or lesser (De Tracy in the second) parts in Oliver's life. Evie, Sergeant Babbacombe's daughter and thus irremediably lower-class, is the most obvious victim of social prejudice. As in *Pincher Martin, Free Fall,* and *The Spire,* male lust reduces a female to a sexual object. Already fair game by virtue of her lowly social status, the much abused Evie is never treated as a full human being by her various male exploiters. To Oliver, her lover, she is no more than "the accessible thing," to be used at his convenience. Momentarily fearing that Evie may be pregnant, Oliver wastes no sympathy on her; rather he is terrified at the prospect of being forced into a socially ruinous marriage. What little vitality exists in socially moribund Stilbourne seems incarnated in Evie who exudes "the breathlessness of perpetual sex"; but whatever love Oliver is capable of feeling is reserved for the upper-middle-class but unattainable Imogen. The marriage of the vain Imogen to the supercilious Norman Claymore perfectly epitomizes the banality of the Stilbourne social ideal. An Evie can never achieve the social security of an Imogen. Although the sergeant's daughter's endless exploitation by men and boys can be read as sexist, it originates in class prejudice. That Bobby Ewan, the doctor's son, "couldn't take the daughter of Sergeant Babbacombe to a dance in his father's car" is instinctively understood — and blandly accepted — by Oliver. And Oliver, the son of a dispensing pharmacist who depends upon Dr. Ewan for his livelihood, treats Evie no less cavalierly. Manifestly below the Ewans on the Stilbourne social pyramid, Oliver and his parents are nonetheless "entitled" to feel contempt for those below them even as they defer to their superiors. Evie's fate, at least so long as she remains in Stilbourne, is determined by an invidious class consciousness as fossilized in the townspeople as it is, despite his raging against it, in Golding himself. "You never loved me, nobody never loved me," cries Evie, her double negatives impressing the snobbish Oliver more than her plea for kindness. Such discordant love is invariably accompanied by disharmonious music. Oliver's unbalanced piano playing relies on a strong left hand to counter a weak right one; his violin playing is hardly more inspired. The disharmonious fiasco of *The King of Hearts* features the gnat-like singing voice of Norman Claymore. Of course the sweet voice of Evie will never be heard in the class-ridden precinct of the Stilbourne Operatic Society.

A plaything to Bobby Ewan and Oliver, Evie is also the object of male fantasies more sinister than theirs. The impotent Captain Wilmot derives what sexual satisfaction he can from beating her. Dr. Jones seduces her under cover of a teacher-pupil arrangement similar to the one she had with Wilmot. The respectable titles of both men testify to their hypocrisy and to that of the society they represent. Of all the perversions of love endured by Evie, the most terrible was an incestuous violation by her brutal father who continues to beat her. It is not until her final meeting with Oliver, two years after his departure for Oxford and hers for London, when Evie inadvertently reveals the incest, that she "suddenly acquired the attributes of a person rather than a thing." Too late Oliver realizes that "I might — *we* might — have made something, music, perhaps, to take the place of the necessary, the inevitable battle." In his emphatic *"we,"* which invokes the musical harmony that might displace the "inevitable battle" (of the sexes? of the classes? of both?) Oliver achieves his finest moment.

Neither love nor music, much less any alliance of the two, achieves real harmony in *The Pyramid.* Powerless to offset chemistry — its symbolic antithesis — music, progressively drained of its harmonies, becomes ironic, discordant, or both. Love, music's putative ally, is equally powerless against the forces of social convention. Thus the inscriptions associated with the novel's two most important women came to nothing. *Amor vincit omnia,* inscribed on Evie's cross, should be revised in Stilbourne where love patently does not conquer all. "Heaven is music," inscribed on Miss Dawlish's gravestone, is no less misleading, associated as it is with a woman whose life in music has been hell. Significantly, both inscriptions ironically testify to the dominance of fathers and the consequent perversion of love. Sergeant Babbacombe's violation of his daughter is a hideous version of *Amor vincit omnia;* and Miss Dawlish's father forcibly channeled her life to accord with "Heaven is music," his own motto. Instituted by fathers and increasingly linked to class consciousness, male dominance becomes the determinant factor in their lives. Evie, notes Oliver when he encounters her again in Stilbourne, "had hitched herself up a couple of degrees on our dreadful ladder." Yet she has essentially reenacted in London the role that had been assigned to her in Stilbourne by becoming the mistress of her boss. And if the beautiful Evie can at least turn female subservience to social advantage, the dowdy Miss Dawlish only loses by her exploitation. Henry Williams, the itinerant young Welsh mechanic with whom Miss Dawlish falls in love, plays upon her affection to secure his raison d'être: social advancement. Along with a "quite unforeseen wife and child," he moves into Miss Dawlish's house after her father's death. Although the money she invests in Henry's family and business is presumably repaid with interest, her investment of love is lost. Even after the prosperous Williamses move out years later, Miss Dawlish continues to bid pathetically for Henry's attention by staging car accidents and, most desperately, by parading naked through Stilbourne. Her frustrated love, repressed sexuality, and sporadic madness, like Henry's rags-to-riches success story and Stilbourne's scandalized notice of their living arrangements, are products of obsessive class consciousness.

A class-ridden society is predictably a voyeuristic one. Ever vigilant if not to prevent at least to censure any violation of, or even mild threat to, social propriety, the self-righteous people of Stilbourne make surveillance a moral imperative. Oliver's mother tirelessly peers out from behind curtained windows; Sergeant Babbacombe relentlessly scours the town in search of his wayward daughter; most egregiously of all, Oliver's father spies through binoculars on his son and Evie making love on the escarpment. Evie's insistence on this public site for their lovemaking exposes the compulsive secrecy and hypocrisy of Stilbourne in general and of Oliver in particular. By setting her own terms for love, Evie temporarily reverses the pattern of male dominance and forces Oliver, again temporarily, to abandon his habitual furtiveness. As deliberately exhibitionistic as Miss Dawlish's public nudity, Evie's open lovemaking likewise opposes the inhibited sexuality of Stilbourne. Typifying the town's attitude is Oliver's father's reaction to the lovemaking he has just spied through his binoculars. In reflexively coupling sex and disease and especially in an outburst that is as revealing as it is uncharacteristic of this reticent man, Oliver's father denounces "this sex — it's *wrong, wrong, wrong!*" Not unexpectedly, he devotes this single display of emotional energy to denial rather than to affirmation. Within a repressive society whose stultifying atmosphere evokes the airless confines of a pyramid, the flagrant displays of Evie and Miss Dawlish are positive statements. That the two women emulate the behavior of Golding's much-admired Egyptians who "do everything in public that other people do in private, and everything in private that other people do in public" may further valorize their taboo-shattering gestures.[8]

Although such gestures are important in themselves they are chiefly valuable for their impact on Oliver, since despite its social satire *The Pyramid* is essentially an initiation story. (Golding's dedication of the novel to his son may be a subtle reminder of its central motif.) In *The Pyramid,* as in many of its twentieth-century counterparts, the modus operandi of the innocence-to-experience scenario is sexual. Because Oliver is the product of Stilbourne — "a loveless society" — his initiation must consist as much of unlearning as learning. What he must unlearn or at least mitigate is the baleful influence of a society "in which it is difficult to love, though not impossible." While the failure of love in Stilbourne is predictable, it is not inevitable because "the class society is a function of the people."[9] Thus the individual may overcome social conditioning by following the advice of Ptah-Hotep, the Egyptian source of *The Pyramid*'s epigraph: "If thou be among people make for thyself love, the beginning and end of the heart." Unfortunately, what happens in *The Pyramid* is that those who would follow the epigraph are powerless to do so. Evie, De Tracy, and Miss Dawlish pathetically, even comically, fail to achieve love. From their various failures Oliver acquires the bits and pieces of knowledge that add up to self-discovery at the end of *The Pyramid.* Ironically, it is not his sexual initiation, an experience conventionally foregrounded in stories of young men growing up, that chiefly contributes to the learning process. Rather it is in his parting conversation with Evie; in his brief encounter with De Tracy; and finally in his return to Stilbourne as a middle-aged man that the lessons of failed love impress themselves most deeply on Oliver.

Each of the three movements of *The Pyramid* concludes in an epiphany of insight that greatly enhances Oliver's awareness of other people and of himself. The first culminates in his perceiving the "undiscovered person" in Evie and his own share in her spoliation. The second consists almost entirely of the farcical preparation and production of the Stilbourne Operatic Society's *King of Hearts*. While the various prejudices and pettinesses of class society are thus spotlighted, they are by this time glaringly obvious to Oliver. A scherzo according to Golding, this second of three sonata movements traditionally quickens musical time to achieve a sprightly and/or humorous effect. Two-thirds of the movement conforms nicely to scherzo expectations; the ensuing interplay between Oliver and De Tracy does not dispel its light tone but darkly counterpoints it. Through De Tracy's eyes, Oliver not only perceives the truth about the "divine" Imogen — "stupid, insensitive, vain" — but also how she incarnates the phony values of Stilbourne hilariously mirrored in the *King of Hearts*. Further, in his treatment of De Tracy Oliver implements the lesson Evie taught. Although he remains comically unaware of the director's homosexual intentions and unintentionally ridicules the photograph of a younger De Tracy in drag, Oliver unfailingly treats him as a person. In running after the hopelessly drunk De Tracy — "the man to whom I now owed so much" — and putting him on the last bus out of Stilbourne, Oliver displays the solicitude wanting in his relationship with Evie. "Evelyn," shouts Oliver after De Tracy's disappearing bus, much as he had cried "Evie" after her departing figure. Teachers of the heart's lessons, Evie and De Tracy remain essentially undiscovered by Oliver. After they recede from sight in the parting scenes that end the first two movements, Oliver is left standing alone in Stilbourne. Whether his own eventual escape owes something to theirs is unclear. What is clear is that one can hardly remain in Stilbourne, even as briefly as De Tracy does, without succumbing to its oppressive air. "I go back on Tuesday," Evie informs Oliver on the Saturday night of their last encounter. "Hold my breath till then." Evie and De Tracy, "whose need to escape is so desperate" that he spends most of his ten-guinea fee on gin, survive their stay in Stilbourne by narcotizing themselves with drink. Both are drunk when they part with Oliver.

The third of Golding's trio of unlucky lovers — Miss Dawlish — is the most tragic. Unlike Evie and De Tracy — and Oliver himself — who simply get out of town, Miss Dawlish can escape the Stilbourne environment only in madness and death. The public imperturbability, expressed in the jaunty walk that earned her the nickname Bounce, masks the private desperation of a woman who struggles long and unsuccessfully for love. Growing up in Stilbourne Oliver was as oblivious to the real Bounce as he was to the real Evie or the real De Tracy. At issue in his return is whether the now middle-aged husband, father, and affluent businessman possesses any more insight than his callow former self. Seated at Bounce's grave, Oliver chiefly remembers how she had discouraged his interest in music: "Don't be a musician...go into the garage business if you want to make money." More than boyhood fear of the domineering Bounce and her gloomy house, it is her sardonic and dismissive advice that leads Oliver to conclude that what everyone assumed to be his devotion to the music teacher was actually hatred. Yet his recollection of the advice that coupled him with Henry Williams, combined with his discovery of the burnt music that reveals Bounce's bottomless despair, triggers the final epiphany of *The Pyramid*. Bounce was right, after all, to perceive the scientist not the musician; to intuit the man in the features of the boy; in short, to understand the Henry Williams in Oliver. In the "same instant" of wishing that he had had the "power of choosing the future" — "I would pay anything — *anything*" — Oliver knows that "like Henry, I would never pay more than a reasonable price." To realize that he, like Henry, is unwilling or unable to pay the price of love is to achieve, however belatedly, the self-knowledge that is the end of initiation.

But the satisfactory working out of *The Pyramid*'s initiation motif lacks the resonance of Golding's previous thematic resolutions. Perhaps this is because Oliver's is an essentially negative epiphany, a perception of stasis rather than a prescription for change. Like the lesser epiphanies invoked by Evie and De Tracy, the shock of recognition Oliver experiences with Henry — "I looked him in the eye; and I saw my own face" — leads nowhere. Notwithstanding its serious topic, the generally comic tone of *The Pyramid* suggests that its issues, like its protagonist, lack their customary power. From *Lord of the Flies* through *The Spire* Golding's novels resonate with cosmic significance. Even in *Free Fall*, whose contemporary mise-en-scène and treatment of aberrant or withheld love recur in *The Pyramid*, God is omnipresent. Despite the secular context of *Free Fall* its stakes are eschatological: Sammy Mountjoy faces salvation or damnation. What ultimately restricts the significance of *The Pyramid* is the effective absence of any viable counter to Evelyn De Tracy's view of life: "It's an outrageous farce, Oliver, with an incompetent producer."

"The Scorpion God"

The comedy of *The Pyramid* broadens in the tales collected in *The Scorpion God*. All three are anthropological fables, tongue-in-cheek send-ups of history that treat change — not, cautions Golding, evolution, which "implies progress in one direction or another" — as largely accidental. Whatever unity the book possesses is, like the events the individual stories depict, "one of the accidents of history." That historical patterns need be neither moral nor rational much less conventionally progressive is a familiar Golding premise embodied most powerfully in *The Inheritors*.[10] Still, despite Golding's disclaimer, the novellas share not only remote settings, surface comicality, and chary historicism but also "the issue of governance or control over a society and the familiar tension between the rational and the mysterious."[11] In the title story, for example, the moribund God-ruler, Great House, represents the waning power of religious governance with its attendant mysteries. His displacement by the Liar, the incarnation of reason, is as disturbing as it is historically predictable. Although the Liar is actually a truth teller, whose name derives from the ignorance of tradition-bound provincials, his accession to power is a mixed blessing. As a representative of "advanced" (i.e., Western) civilization — an "outlander with his own fantasies" — the Liar subverts the received wisdom of a hermetic society. At the same time he reflects Golding's usual ambivalence about the Darwinian concept of the survival of the fittest. The Liar's defeat of the Head Man, who incarnates the prestige of the priesthood and exercises effective political control, represents social but not necessarily moral evolution. By dismantling the traditional network of loyalties and obligations the Liar substitutes personal assertion for group consensus. When he is thrown into the pit, he does not scruple to survive at the expense of the blind old man whose food and water he appropriates. And his appeals to the princess, Pretty Flower, are based chiefly on mutual lust. Emulating Homo sapiens of *The Inheritors* whose annihilation of the Neanderthals likewise epitomizes the victory of guile over innocence, the Liar defeats his more ignorant and less ruthless adversaries. With the death of the Head Man at the hands of the Liar the old order passes, giving way to the new. What this new dispensation promises is heralded by the Liar's rejection of eternal life — "Because this one is good enough" — and with it the entire otherworldly panoply of an ingenuous and superstitious society. His shocking declaration is "the awful thing, the dirty thing, the thing that broke up the world."

For a hereditary and hierarchical order, spawned, sustained, and symbolized by incestuous sex, the Liar would substitute a putative meritocracy. His nonincestuous lovemaking with Pretty Flower shatters the sexual taboo that preserved the status quo. Combined with his refusal to be buried with Great House and thereby to achieve eternal life, this "unnatural" sex act symptomizes a worldview diametrically opposed to the existent one. It is only a short step to the ultimate blasphemy of self-sanctification: "*Supposing I were Great House?*" the Liar asks of the Head Man in the voice of "a God." The Head Man resembles Mal, the Neanderthal elder and leader of *The Inheritors*, in knowing as much as his society affords. And like Mal he is helpless to withstand the impact of superior knowledge. "What a man can know, I know" boasts the Head Man to Pretty Flower, invoking "reason" to expose the Liar's geographical "fictions": "Suppose for a moment the sky to be so big it stretched out to cover these lands! Well — think of the weight." Not only do his words betray the restricted visual field of the Head Man; they also go a long way toward justifying the Liar. What began ostensibly as a clash between faith and reason turns out to be a clash between "reason" and reason. The Liar does not so much repudiate the religious impulse as redirect it. And even if this is nothing more than another version of the rationalism that Golding distrusts, it is patently superior to that of the Head Man. Significantly, the novella's conclusion portrays a sexually recharged Pretty Flower, her arms extended in a "gesture reserved for revelation," approaching the Liar to "talk to Him." His self-deification validated by the capitalization of Pretty Flower's awed "Him," the Liar will presumably inherit Great House's place at her side and in her bed, thus promulgating a new and more potent dynasty. That his empowerment is a positive development may be inferred not only from the affirmative ending. For the deified Liar of "The Scorpion God" becomes the avatar of that Egypt to which Golding is so magnetically drawn: "I choose to make the scorpion Pharaoh the one who unites the whole of Egypt, so when the dying high priest says 'he stings like a scorpion', that names the Pharaoh. He is going to unite Egypt, make it a great power.... And so he is Scorpion, and he is God."[12]

"Clonk Clonk"

The primeval world of "Clonk Clonk" evokes the lost Eden of *The Inheritors*. Like the Neanderthals, the prehistoric African tribespeople of "Clonk Clonk" are prelapsarians whose lives are attuned to nature's rhythms. The differentiated but complementary roles of the sexes, the matrilineal values, and the communal solidarity of people who sleep like a "mass of skin and togetherness" additionally recall Neanderthal society. Unlike the Neanderthals, however, whose biorhythms are fatally disrupted by encroaching Homo sapiens, the African tribe faces little threat to its natural harmony, much less to its continued existence. Luckily for the tribespeople of "Clonk Clonk," who share the Neanderthal's limited mental capacity, no Homo sapiens appears to take advantage of their vulnerability. Thus Chimp momentarily feels the same loneliness that afflicted his counterpart, Lok, in *The Inheritors:* "A problem was all round him and through him but he had no word for it, nothing was like it, he had never had a problem to solve before. He was neither sick nor old; but he was alone." Chimp's fear and the syntax of its expression would be equally at home in *The Inheritors.* But in *The Inheritors* Lok's trepidation prefigures his — and his people's — annihilation, while in "Clonk Clonk" Chimp "was safe though he had no way of knowing it." Primeval social harmony is shattered in *The Inheritors,* preserved in "Clonk Clonk." Matriarchal values, incarnated in the graceful and gracious Palm, hold in check the aggressive and competitive instincts of the males. Instituted in Palm's unquestioned leadership, matriarchal dominance is the key to the happy ending of "Clonk Clonk." Because the more intelligent women perform all the essential functions of the society, men are necessary only for propagation. Even their habitual hunting expeditions are as inessential as they are often unproductive, since the women already supply the staple diet of eggs and fish. Intellectually and emotionally children, the males instinctively accept the benevolent female hegemony that ensures social harmony and stability. The subordinate status of men is reflected in their names that, unlike those of women, constantly change. Chimp, for example, is first introduced as Charging Elephant; several name changes later he ends the novella as Wounded Leopard. The final name signals his acceptance as Palm's husband and his reintegration with the Leopard Men. His days as Chimp, the social outcast, safely behind him,

Wounded Leopard joins in the celebration of communal well-being: "So everything ended happily and all changes were for the best."

"Envoy Extraordinary"

This isn't necessarily so in "Envoy Extraordinary" where Caesar believes that "changes are almost always for the worse." Coincidentally, the theme of change is reflected not only in the subject matter but in the publishing history of the novella. "Envoy Extraordinary" began life as a story (1956) only to be dramatized, first as a radio play for the BBC, then as a full-length play — *The Brass Butterfly* — performed at London's Strand Theatre (1958). Finally it resumed its original form and title as the last of the three novellas in *The Scorpion God* (1971). In "Envoy Extraordinary" the spokesman for change is Phanocles, a destitute Greek inventor, who claims that with Caesar's help "I can change the universe." Like the Liar in "The Scorpion God," Phanocles is ahead of his time. Both are rationalists dedicated to shattering the sustaining myths of the past. "Poetry, magic, religion" — the epistemological tools of the ancient world — evoke false images of a universe which, according to Phanocles, is nothing more than "a machine." Like Golding's other literal-minded scientists, the Greek inventor is an ambivalent figure. Phanocles is unquestionably devoted to improving the human condition; but he is blind to the potentially harmful consequences of scientific advancement, believing simply that progress is its own justification. Although the Roman Emperor's Platonic humanism can be as exasperatingly one-dimensional as the Greek inventor's scientific rationalism, Caesar's characterization of Phanocles is apposite: "Your single-minded and devoted selflessness, your royal preoccupation with the only thing that can interest you, could go near to wiping life off the earth."

Of the three inventions Phanocles proffers to Caesar, only

the pressure cooker excites the Emperor's unqualified enthusiasm. Although the steamship and explosive missile contribute to the destruction of Posthumus and the failure of his coup attempt, they are rejected by Caesar who foresees that their death-dealing potential is ultimately uncontrollable. Phanocles consoles himself with the hope that political evolution will bring about a day "when men are free" and when his "greatest inventions" will no longer prove dangerous. Caesar dismisses this as the pipe dream of a political idealist too naive to understand that slavery will persist "though the name may change," since the "domination of the weak by the strong" is neverending. It is this subtle thematic shift from the scientific to the moral ramifications of change that momentarily subverts the predominantly comic tone of "Envoy Extraordinary." Characteristically, Golding's moral conclusion relates to the innate depravity of human nature. This is revealed most explicitly in the dialogue of *The Brass Butterfly*:

PHANOCLES: Caesar, I conquered the universe, and yet the ants have defeated me. What is wrong with man?

CAESAR: Men. A steam ship, or anything powerful in the hands of man, Phanocles, is like a sharp knife in the hands of a child. There is nothing wrong with the knife. There is nothing wrong with the steam ship. There is nothing wrong with man's intelligence. The trouble is his nature.

"Envoy Extraordinary" regains its comic equilibrium at the end when Caesar, initially enthusiastic about printing, rejects this latest invention of Phanocles. Horrified at the prospect of a future world inundated by worthless books and trivial information, the Emperor "rewards" Phanocles by packing him off as ambassador to China.

The three novellas of *The Scorpion God* and *The Pyramid* invoke many of the important moral issues contained in Golding's previous books. Yet the slighter structures and lighter tone of the two later works seem designed to sidestep the profound personal struggles and grave consequences of their predecessors. If the conventional two-part division of Golding's career is accepted, then *The Spire* (1964) concludes act 1 and *Darkness Visible* (1979) begins act 2. Between the acts come *The Pyramid* and *The Scorpion God,* Golding not dissonant but in a minor key.

8

Fire Sermon: *Darkness Visible*

Darkness Visible (1979) breaks an unusually long silence for Golding, who needed only three or four months to write *Lord of the Flies* and only one month apiece for *The Inheritors* and *Pincher Martin*.[1] His first fiction in eight years, *Darkness Visible* was also Golding's first novel in twelve years; and given the piecemeal publication of *The Pyramid*, *Darkness Visible* could legitimately be regarded as the novelistic successor to *The Spire* (1964). In any event, *Darkness Visible* resonates with the cosmic significance pervasive in the first five novels but largely missing from *The Pyramid* and *The Scorpion God*. Its long gestation suggests the difficulty of finding the appropriate contemporary context in which to reexplore the darkness of human nature. A quarter of a century after *Lord of the Flies*, *Darkness Visible* invokes the identical moral concerns of Golding's first novel in an expanded and updated setting. Its opening apocalyptic scene of a world ablaze eerily recalls the flaming island at the end of *Lord of the Flies*. In both novels, fire evokes the generic hell of the human condition in the particular hell of World War II. It was the war that stripped Golding of his belief "in the perfectibility of social man" and left him with the conviction that man was "a morally diseased creation."[2] On the evidence of *Darkness Visible*, the pessimism Golding once characterized as temporary seems permanently implanted. Whereas, however, *Lord of the Flies* ends in despair, *Darkness Visible* allows the possibility of redemption.

That possibility is incarnated in the child who mysteriously emerges from the "great fire" of the London Blitz. Matty's survival — "Nor do small children walk out of a fire that is melting lead and distorting iron" — is so miraculous as to suggest "the Apocalypse." The richly evocative fire imagery attending his appearance invests Matty and the "ferociously consumed" world with a supernatural aura. Although that world is 1940 London, it is essentially timeless. Matty, a "flickering brightness," materializes from a "burning bush" like the one from which God spoke to Moses in *Exodus*. London, bathed in a "shameful, inhuman light," has become "a version of the infernal city" embodied in the title and epigraph of *Darkness Visible*. The title — describing Hell in book 1 of Milton's *Paradise Lost* — and the epigraph — preceding the descent of Aeneas and the Sybil into the underworld in book 6 of Virgil's *Aeneid* — together with biblical allusions to the Apocalypse invoke a modern chiaroscuro. In its interplay of light and darkness, the opening scene of *Darkness Visible* establishes the symbolic referents of Golding's Manichean vision of the world.

Golding's "infernal city" may also owe something to T. S. Eliot's London — the "Unreal City" of *The Waste Land*. Like the poem, whose title has become nearly a clichéd synonym for the modern age, *Darkness Visible* anatomizes a fallen civilization in the aftermath of world war. Golding follows Eliot not only in setting forth conditions for redemption but in relating them to the purgatorial cleansing of fire. While it is true that water rather than fire is the controlling metaphor of *The Waste Land*, the poem's central section is entitled "The Fire Sermon" and ends with the word *burning*. According to Eliot, the invocation of Buddha in the title and of St. Augustine in the ending unites "two representatives of eastern and western asceticism." And like Buddha and St. Augustine, Matty incarnates in asceticism a purifying fire. Eliot's fire imagery is even more pronounced in the final two sections of "Little Gidding," the last of his *Four Quartets*, where redemption, desired in vain in *The Waste Land*, is finally achieved. In the penultimate fourth section of "Little Gidding," Eliot fuses air

raid and Christian imagery in a "flame of incandescent terror." A similar fusion is apparent in the no less evocative fire
imagery that illuminates the first scene of *Darkness Visible*.
Matty, *from* the fire and *of* the fire, embodies Eliot's formula:
"To be redeemed from fire by fire." The phrase could serve
as easily in *Darkness Visible* as a description of Matty's fate
and an epitaph for Sebastian Pedigree. It is just before his own
death that Pedigree sees the already-dead Matty "consumed,
melted, vanished like a guy in a bonfire." Exiting the novel as
he had entered it, Matty appears in fire to confer on Pedigree
the freedom of death. As in "Little Gidding," fire may either
damn the sinner burning like Pedigree with lust or save him by
burning away the impure element. Matty is the purifying fire,
releasing Pedigree from the consuming rage of his own inner
fires. Ending in fire as it began, *Darkness Visible* is ultimately a
dramatization of the couplet that concludes the fourth section
of "Little Gidding:" "We only live, only suspire / Consumed
by either fire or fire."

Matty's composite makeup suggests the ambivalence of
human nature. The fire spares the right side of his face but
leaves the left hideously disfigured. He is at once everyman
and no man. Because he has "no background but the fire," he
is first called "number seven" and then Matthew Septimus.
The specificity of these Christian names is belied, however,
by the vagueness of his assigned surname — Windrove. Endlessly confused by everyone he meets, the shifting surname
(Windup, Windrop, etc.) emphasizes the arbitrariness of his
identity and his essential anonymity in the eyes of others.
At the Foundlings School in the ironically named Greenfield
Village, Matty's identity is predictably determined by his dis-
figurement. The butt of his classmates' cruel jokes, he begins
to comprehend the alienating effect of his deformity, an effect compounded by the inarticulateness whose symbols are
a missing left ear and misshapen mouth. Matty's hideous appearance provokes the disgust of Sebastian Pedigree, a closet
homosexual addicted to the pretty boys, notably Henderson, who pass through his classroom. Sarcastically called "a

treasure" by the schoolmaster, Matty mistakes Pedigree's revulsion for affection. His subsequent devotion to Pedigree springs from the same literal-mindedness that causes Matty to tattle on his schoolmates. When his poorly concealed sexual preferences prompt a warning from the headmaster, the nervous Pedigree begins conducting private tutorials with the hated Matty instead of the beloved Henderson. This subterfuge backfires, deepening Matty's love and precipitating Henderson's death. Whether Henderson's fatal fall from the school roof is suicidal or accidental, it plays a critically formative role in the lives of Pedigree and Matty. When Matty's gym shoe is inexplicably found beneath Henderson's body, Pedigree takes it as evidence of complicity in his favorite's death. The schoolmaster's words of blame — "You horrible, horrible boy! It's all your fault" — sear Matty's psyche as the fire seared his face. Again the literal-minded Matty takes the words of his trusted friend as gospel. Pedigree's parting cry haunts Matty, imbuing him with a sense of guilt and sinfulness and forming spiritual scars as permanent as his physical ones. While Pedigree suffers dismissal, imprisonment, and an isolation ultimately as profound as Matty's, it is, of course, he who has betrayed Matty and not vice versa as the boy erroneously believes.

That Matty takes upon himself the guilt that rightly belongs to Pedigree confirms and extends the symbolic identity implicit in his mysterious origin. As everyman Matty bears the burden of original sin and shares, albeit obliquely, the responsibility for Henderson's death. The Old Testament curse — "Over Edom have I cast out my shoe" — pronounced by Matty as he flung his gym shoe toward the spot where Henderson would fall to his death, reveals both the wish for the rival's destruction and the eerie spiritual power to effect it. At the same time, Matty acts in the conviction that he is expelling the "Evil" that Pedigree teasingly attributed to Henderson and that Matty, as usual, takes literally. Despite his representative status as a character whose outward appearance and inner conflict epitomize man's double nature, Matty is distinguished chiefly by his singular rather than typical attributes. It is as one of Gold-ing's saints that he figures so prominently in *Darkness Visible*. Whereas his Christlike counterparts such as Simon in *Lord of the Flies* and Nat in *Pincher Martin* were relatively pas-sive and ineffectual supporting actors, Matty is empowered by a greatly expanded role. Of all Golding's unworldly holy fools it is Matty who is most strikingly and consistently identi-fied with Christ. In his miraculous birth, willing self-sacrifice, holy visions, affinity with the cross, spear wounds that re-semble stigmata, reappearance (resurrection?) after death in response to Pedigree's cry for help, even in his speech — "the innocent language of the spirit. The language of paradise" — Matty imitates Christ. And Golding's relentlessly biblical con-text foregrounds numerous episodes in which Matty reenacts the life of Christ. Like Christ, Matty is cast out and perse-cuted; but his sufferings, unlike Christ's, are susceptible to ironic interpretation. Australia, where Matty goes in penance for his imagined sin and in search of himself and his purpose in life, is the scene of physical and spiritual trials that approx-imate Christ's in form if not always in substance. Wandering in what he takes to be a wilderness but is actually the sub-urbs of Darwin, Matty encounters "scrubby thorns" and a "low hump of three trees." There he is set upon by Harry Bummer, a disaffected Aboriginal whose hatred of whites is exacerbated by the cross Matty has drawn with pebbles. To Bummer the cross is not only a sign of the white man's religion but a signal to British airplanes to begin nuclear testing in Aus-tralia. "Fucking big sky-fella him b'long Jesus Christ!" shouts the enraged Abo, nearly emasculating the innocent Matty by jumping on his groin after first spearing his "open palm." "Crucified," Matty mumbles to the good Samaritan in the guise of a passing veterinarian who gives him water, binds up his genitals, and delivers him to a Darwin hospital. The en-tire episode typifies Matty's simultaneous identification with, and parody of, Christ. Thus the stab wounds are "no more than scratches," according to the ministering veterinarian: "crucifarce or crucifiction."

Whatever their biblical coloration, Matty's experiences in England and Australia, crystallized respectively in the Greenfield and Darwin episodes, spotlight his role as victim. The quintessential outsider, separated from humanity by his fearful appearance and habitual silence, he is further isolated by the neutered sexuality symbolized by his near castration by the Abo. Drawn towards girls — "His sexuality . . . was in direct proportion to his unattractiveness" — he soon comes to realize that sexual fulfillment, much less marriage, is impossible. At Frankley's, where he runs menial errands after being expelled from the Foundlings School as uneducable, Matty is moved by the half-seen face of an attractive girl. But "he had become aware" that "his unattractive appearance would have made an approach to the girl into a farce and humiliation"; and "that it would be so with any woman." Grief "for a vanished prospect" and guilt for his imagined offense against Pedigree converge to trigger Matty's self-exile from England. It is in flight from the tempting but unattainable "daughters of men" and the "impossibility of healing Pedigree" that Matty goes "as far as humanly possible." Yet "Pedigree's cause came with him" even to Australia; Matty leaves his first job when it is "rendered unspeakably dangerous by a girl both pretty and painted." Not only has he failed to outdistance his troubles, but the linkage between sex and guilt has strengthened. Without deluding himself that any woman would have him, he nonetheless imagines that he "must offer up marriage, sex, love" to atone for having "injured" his "only friend."

The conjunction of sex and guilt in *Darkness Visible* reflects Golding's belief in original sin and his tendency to represent it in acts of sexual bad faith. Whether aggressive, aberrant, or repressed, sexuality contributes powerfully to the human sinfulness omnipresent in his novels. Pedigree's is manifest in the homosexual preference for young boys that leads, at least indirectly, to Henderson's death and his own disgrace. Given the unhappy role of sex in Golding's work, Pedigree's fate is hardly an indictment of homosexuality. Rather it is another of the many instances of sexuality serving as a metaphor for human depravity. In the blighted sexual context of *Darkness Visible* — typical of Golding's representations of modernity — Matty's successful repression of his erotic instincts may be a positive achievement. An aspect of his early perception that, lacking "defences," he had "no remedy but simply to endure," sexual continence completes his retreat into a self-imposed silence. Whether the progressive stages of Matty's isolation constitute a conscious strategy of endurance or a rationalization after the fact, they unquestionably enhance his spiritual receptivity. More and more he turns to scripture for the consolations unavailable to him via human intercourse. Biblical immersion leads to mystical revelations that, like his various imitations of Christ, are as ironic as they are ingenuous. It is significant that just before his sexuality is symbolically, perhaps even literally, destroyed by the Abo, Matty remembers a "horrible" biblical quotation — *"Some have made themselves eunuchs for the sake of the kingdom of God."* That this particular passage should occur to him may express his buried longing for the impotence that would permanently extinguish the fires of lust. While it is not necessary to read wish fulfillment into the Abo's assault on Matty's genitals, it is nonetheless true that it provides the desired, if paradoxical, release.

Whatever its precise significance, the "crucifarce" lends urgency to Matty's struggle toward self-definition. Key to the spiritual quest that began in earnest when he reached Australia, the question of personal identity is reformulated by Matty after his ordeal. "Who am I?" had already become "What am I?" and now becomes "What am I for?" — the "burning question" that can be asked but not answered in Australia. Matty's time in Australia, like the exile of the prophet Ezekiel with whom he explicitly identifies, is an incubator for revelation. Ezekiel's warning to the Israelites inspires Matty's tower of matchboxes whose "great flame licked across the wasteland." The secretary who rebukes him for starting a dangerous fire nevertheless rightly interprets it as a prediction of "calamity" in the event that the British continue the "meteorological gamble" of testing atomic bombs in Australia. The matchbox fire does more than reveal Matty's prophetic calling — the apparent answer to his "What am I for?" Fire, the transcendent metaphor of *Darkness Visible,* is Matty's destiny as well as his métier. Even as it establishes his function it recalls his beginning and prefigures his end.

A last symbolic action is required of Matty in preparation for returning to England where he will take up his prophetic work and where his warnings are needed more than in Australia. As if to underline the ritual nature of Matty's nighttime descent into "low down" marshy water, "hot and fetid," Golding changes the narrative focus. Matty becomes "the driver," "the man" who, holding aloft an antique lamp and weighted down with "heavy steel wheels" slung from a "chain round his waist," sinks into the muddy waters "with unutterable pain." The altered point of view lasts only as long as the immersion ritual, effectively setting it off as with quotation marks. A similar use of narrative distancing as a transition device occurred in *The Inheritors* when Lok began his passage from life to death. Although Matty's passage from Australia to England eventuates in his death, his ritual immersion is less a rehearsal for dying than a preparation for prophesying. Another effect of temporarily displacing Matty as the novel's central consciousness is to obscure his purpose, which from the newly objective viewpoint seems "incomprehensible" or "inscrutable." Matty's watery rite of passage suggests baptism with its overtones of purification, sanctification, and initiation — likely prerequisites for prophesying. His curious choice of wheels as weights seems designed to invoke Matty's role model — the prophet Ezekiel — as do Golding's several references to the "creatures" of the water. One of the most striking passages in the Old Testament Book of Ezekiel repeatedly juxtaposes "living creatures" and the wheels that contain their spirit: "for the spirit of the creatures was in the wheels" (Ezekiel 1:21). From this moment, when the heavens opened and "the hand of the Lord came upon him," Ezekiel is empowered to prophesy doom to the Israelites. Not for the first or the last time in *Darkness Visible* does Matty consciously or subconsciously invoke Ezekiel to validate his own prophetic calling. Because his investiture as prophet marks the beginning of a new life, Matty's descent into the "even darker darkness" of the marsh and subsequent rise from its clinging "ooze" are symbolic of death and rebirth. And because the "faint phosphorescence," wandering "flames," flashing "sparks," and "cloud of fire" evoke the darkness visible of Hell, Matty has apparently reenacted the epic descent into the underworld. *Sit mihi fas audita loqui* — the epigraph to *Darkness Visible* — begins Aeneas's prayer to the gods for permission "to disclose / things buried in the dark and deep / of earth!" Matty, like Aeneas, returns from the underworld possessed of hidden mysteries and fortified to pursue his destiny.

Even if Matty's descent enacts nothing more than the febrile imaginings of a limited intelligence steeped in biblical literalism, it is a fitting rehearsal for returning to the hell of mid-1960s England. So hopeless is its condition — trivial, vulgar, clamorous, violent, racially divided — that England seems ripe for the Apocalypse that Matty, on the basis of his readings in the Book of Revelation, is convinced will occur on the sixth day of the sixth month of 1966. When the fatal 6/6/66 passes without incident he feels "the dreadful sorrow of not being in heaven with judgment all done." Still, he infers from the regular visits of a red spirit and a blue spirit that "Great things are afoot." Matty's confidence in the holy identity of his tutelary spirits is sorely tested by their command to throw away his Bible. But overcoming his momentary fear that the spirits are Satan in disguise and casting his Bible into the sea, he passes the trial of faith. That Matty no longer needs the Bible may evidence his mastery of its lessons. If the formerly indispensable Bible is now superfluous he could be ready to eschew biblical literalism for more direct communication with God. Of course Matty's colloquy with the spirits may be hallucinatory, the product of fasting, loneliness, and skewed religiosity. Yet whatever their genesis and actual form, the spirits, whose visits Matty meticulously records in a journal, determine his future course of action. Assured by the spirits that he is "near the centre of things" and instructed by them to journey east from Cornwall, he ends up back in Greenfield. There his fate will be somehow linked to a child's; and he will finally learn the answer to the question, "What am I for?"

Greenfield, Golding's microcosm of fallen England, "is much changed" and more inaptly named than ever. Matty feels "a great desire to prophesy" against a town profaned by a "heathen temple" and a mosque. His Quixote-like entrance into Greenfield on a rickety bicycle — a mode of transportation less convenient and more expensive than the train but one ordained by his spirits — parodies the coming of the Messiah. Yet the very incongruity of his actions, like the grotesqueness of his looks, underlines the plight of England. Although Matty seizes upon the wrong symbols (temple, mosque) of Greenfield's moral degeneracy, it is nonetheless real. Vanished is the communal solidarity, the sense of common purpose that sustained England during the darkest days of World War II. What Hannah Arendt observed in Adolf Eichmann — the banality of evil — is present, albeit mutedly, in 1960s Greenfield. Whether the prewar England that the fire fighters of 1940 saved — along, significantly, with Matty — and that Golding himself skewered in *The Pyramid,* was markedly superior is debatable. But the human feeling that socially stratified Stilbourne repressed seems not to exist at all in amoral and anomic Greenfield. That the state of the modern world as incarnated in Greenfield is perilous is evidenced by Golding's unlikely choice of a redeemer: "You are," the spirits inform Matty, "the best material that can be obtained in the circumstances." To vest redemption in such a figure as Matty not only spotlights England's degeneracy but Golding's pessimism, hardly abated in the quarter century that separates *Darkness Visible* from *Lord of the Flies.* Postwar despair indicts the present as it valorizes the past. Nostalgia for a better (i.e., prior) world is similarly evoked in *The Waste Land* whose moral ambience suggests that of *Darkness Visible.* Spiritually moribund Greenfield recalls the eponymous landscape of T. S. Eliot's poem, a collage of images depicting modern emptiness. In *The Waste Land* redemptive potential is vested in the Fisher King who turns out, however, to be powerless to effect positive change. This ironically impotent fertility figure may be the model for Matty whose outsized but maimed genitals simultaneously evoke and negate his redemptive potency. Although Golding's unlikely redeemer fleetingly irradiates the spiritual lives of skeptical Sim Goodchild and fatuous Edwin Bell and may actually save the soul of pitiful Sebastian Pedigree, Matty ultimately can no more transform Greenfield than the Fisher King could rejuvenate *The Waste Land*.

The sinfulness Matty must contend with is not embodied primarily in Pedigree whose homosexuality invariably victimizes himself more than others. In part 2: Sophy, the "spiritual kingdom" — light — of part 1: Matty is abandoned for the "weird" world — darkness — of the terrible Stanhope sisters. Avatars of evil, the dark Sophy and the fair Toni represent the two faces of natural depravity. The passionately self-absorbed Sophy and the coldly unfeeling Toni together personify contemporary moral entropy. Near the end of *Darkness Visible* Sim Goodchild identifies them with the sorry condition of 1970s England where history has degenerated into "a sprawling series of events that break apart under their own weight." To Goodchild, the vicious criminality of the Stanhope twins, those "lovely creatures" possessed of "everything in the world, youth, beauty, intelligence," suggests that there is "nothing to live for." His sale of his traditional bookshop "to the shopping-centre people" reflects Goodchild's conviction that standards are declining and that everything is running down. Again the betrayed promise and tragic waste that Goodchild (and Golding?) identifies with the 1960s generation is embodied in Sophy and Toni: "A treasure was poured out for them and they turned their back on it. A treasure not just for them but for all of us." That "treasure" is reflected in the twins' outward beauty that conceals their inner darkness much as Matty's disfigured body obscures his inner light.

Sophy and Toni invoke the sixties credo of personal free-dom only to pervert it in acts of wanton violence. Part 2 of *Darkness Visible* focuses on the destructiveness of Sophy who remains in England while Toni drifts off into a career of international terrorism. Sophy's sadism, apparent from early childhood when she hurled a stone at a dabchick and killed it, is expressed most clearly in her sexuality. Only by stabbing Roland in the shoulder during lovemaking does she experience her first orgasm. In this epiphanic moment of sexual fulfill-ment through violence Sophy's identification with darkness, adumbrated in the killing of the dabchick, is sealed: "All at once a world fell into place." To invoke sexual aberrance as a metaphor of evil is nothing new for Golding. It is probably no accident that he reserves his bluntest and fullest treatment of sex for the moral wasteland of *Darkness Visible*. Nor that consummate evil is vested in the sexually active Sophy, re-demptive good in the effectively impotent Matty. Sophy, like Pincher Martin, is little more than the sum of her appetites. And sex is no more for her than a mechanism for imposing her will upon men. Domination and self-gratification converge in her casual loss of virginity; in her taking up with and drop-ping Roland; in her incestuous temptation of her father; and in her "engagement" to Fido as a means of furthering her plot to kidnap an Arab princeling. Although she seems genuinely attracted to Gerry, she soon reduces him and his friend Bill to Fido's status of reluctant accomplice. The plot itself seems purposeless except as an extension of Sophy's will to power through violence. In her fantasy of thrusting a knife into the kidnapped boy and watching his blood flow she relives the epiphany of her first orgasm: "She was trembling with the pas-sion of the mock murder." The ultimate act of self-assertion, this imagined murder fuses sex and violence into an almost ritual celebration of darkness.

Sophy's bizarre kidnapping plot effects the climactic clash between her evil and Matty's good in the concluding third section of *Darkness Visible*. Yet the title of part 3 — "One Is One" — seems to refer less to any single incident than to the condition of spiritual isolation. Greenfield circa 1978 is a microcosm of England in decline, a proving ground for Golding's view that "we are in the age of the fragment and wreckage."[3] In late middle age Sim Goodchild and Edwin Bell, longtime Greenfield residents who remember when "the Green was still a village green," bemoan the vanished past and deplore the diminished present. Though Sim assesses the damage in cultural, Edwin in spiritual, terms, both see symptoms of irreversible decline in the new social order. Greenfield's loss of communal purpose, racial and religious friction, even its relentlessly noisy traffic of cars and jet planes typify the modern wasteland. Worst of all is the bondage of the self that isolates people from one another. Even such old friends as Sim and Edwin communicate only tentatively, justifying Sim's maxim: "One is one and all alone and ever more shall be so." The insulated self is at once the cause and effect of that quintessentially modern phenomenon of alienation: the lonely crowd. In Greenfield as in *The Waste Land,* everyone is, in T. S. Eliot's words, "each in his prison." Alienation fosters spiritual malaise as symbolized by the conversion of a Greenfield church into a community center. Not that there is any sense of community; what communal rapport existed presumably went the way of the faith that once sustained the church. And not coincidentally, the Little Theatre Group rehearses Sartre's play, *Huis Clos (No Exit)*, in "the north transept where they used to reserve the sacrament." In his revealingly titled essay, "Crosses," Golding invokes the people of *Huis Clos* "whose hell it is eternally to torture each other . . . with the sheer pressure of their individual beings." In the last paragraph of "Crosses," Sartre's mise-en-scène symptomizes what "has become a commonplace of this century:" "That a random selection of people can inflict utter cruelty on one another." Encoded in the Greenfield wasteland of *Darkness Visible* this grim scenario has its epilogue in a cheerless future: "It may be that, in a hundred years, the ambition of every sensitive man will be the tranquillity of a hermit's cell."[4]

If exorcising the spiritual malaise endemic to the late twentieth century is aggregatively impossible, it is individually plausible. That the antidote to the meaningless babble of human voices and the bogus camaraderie of community centers is the "wordless communication" of Matty comes as no surprise. Edwin instigates and Sim acquiesces to a séance with Matty that culminates in a momentary revelation of the "ineffable promise" of the "world of spirit." An epiphany of sorts is experienced by Sim after his hand is "read" by Matty: "In a convulsion unlike anything he had ever known, Sim stared into the gigantic world of his own palm and saw that it was holy." The revelation moves even the habitually skeptical Sim to agree with Edwin's assessment of the séance: "We broke a barrier, broke down a partition." It may be more accurate to say that the séance opened a window of opportunity through which Sim and Edwin might glimpse, however fleetingly, a world of spirit beyond the waste of self. Yet until the escape from self can be perpetuated, the barrier may be breached but not broken. An unconditional surrender of the self effected by a leap of faith analogous to but greater than the one inspired by Matty is the prerequisite for spiritual renewal. Capable of self-recognition but incapable of self-transcendence, Sim and Edwin soon sink back into the ranks of the spiritually uncommitted. Matty has touched their lives without transforming them. After Matty's death, Sim "found himself staring intently into his own palm," yet tentative as always. Recollecting the séance, he feels "heartened," even "happy" — but only "for the moment."

Matty fulfills his redemptive destiny not in Sim's momentary enlightenment but in Pedigree's apparent salvation. Christlike, Matty must sacrifice his own life that another may "live." This he does in saving the Arab princeling, an act that can be read either as obedience to his tutelary spirits, expiation for his "sin" against his "friend," or both. In rescuing the child by sacrificing himself to the flames, Matty not only defeats the forces of evil led by Sophy — the Whore of Babylon — but preserves the new Messiah who will "bring the spiritual language into the world." Matty's return as a burnt offering to the fire from whence he came recalls T. S. Eliot's redemptive conclusion to "Little Gidding": "the end of all our exploring / Will be to arrive where we started." What Eliot enjoins Matty has achieved in the course of closing the circle from fire to fire: "A condition of complete simplicity / (Costing not less than everything)." Of all the characters in *Darkness Visible* Matty alone proves able, or willing, to pay Eliot's price — the unconditional surrender of the self — of spiritual serenity. Fittingly, the fire imagery that attended Matty's nativity and effects his apotheosis irradiates the last chapter of the novel. A "strange thing happened," for example, "in the fire" that engulfs Matty: "It seemed to organize itself into a shape of flame." If, as his spirits revealed, Matty's primary mission on earth was to save the holy child, then his fiery transfiguration fills Eliot's prescription for redemption:

> All manner of thing shall be well
> When the tongues of flames are in-folded
> Into the crowned knot of fire.

Matty's imitation of Christ is most convincing, however, not in his rescue of the child but in his redemption of Pedigree. Slumped on a park bench, Pedigree discovers himself "to be sitting up to his very eyes in a sea of light." Toward him weaves the dead Matty, "waist deep in gold." Tears streaming down his face, Pedigree confesses that he had doubted Matty's existence and had tried — unsuccessfully — to throw away Matty's love. In belatedly recognizing that Matty's love can no more be refused than Christ's, and in crying out to Matty for help, the compulsive child molester becomes the humble suppliant. As if in direct response to this cry — the very leap of faith that Sim found impossible — the resurrected Matty vanishes into the flames that swirl about him, only to emerge transfigured. No longer "two-tone but gold as the fire," Matty's face now reflects the essence of his spiritual identity rather than the accident of his physical deformity. Salvation is embodied in his "peacock eyes of great feathers" and "loving and terrible smile." The peacock, whose miraculous beauty incarnates God's creative power, symbolizes the transfigured savior. ("Christ will come like that!" cries the priest in Flannery O'Connor's "The Displaced Person.")

That this saving vision should appear to the likes of Pedigree is no more or less remarkable than that his savior should appear in the transfigured likeness of Matty. Unlikely suppliant and redeemer, this odd couple epitomizes the Christian symbiosis that invokes salvation even in the spiritual wasteland of the late twentieth century. Pedigree, moreover, achieves his finest moment in crying out for help — for himself but equally for the child he may one day kill to silence. Not that he wants to die: "No! No! No!" Pedigree cries out "in agony" as Matty's transfigured face draws closer. Yet in that single instant of praying for an unknown child Pedigree accomplished "The awful daring of a moment's surrender / Which an age of prudence can never retract" — Eliot's precondition for redemption in *The Waste Land*. Saved, *malgré lui,* the "filthy old thing" that the park keeper approaches has been translated into heaven as a soul in bliss. The park keeper's description evokes the usual ambivalence of Golding's endings. Was Pedigree's vision of Matty transfigured and salvation imminent real or hallucinatory? Yet whatever its intimations of Pedigree's ultimate fate, the visionary moment incarnates the possibility, if not the certainty, of redemption.

To opt for the best-case scenario — Matty the savior, Pedigree the saved — is not to expect its inevitable recurrence. Golding offers no evidence that the emblematic spiritual malaise of Greenfield has been dispelled; nor has the Apocalypse Matty so confidently awaited on 6/6/66 come about. Like Christ before him and the Arab child who will perhaps follow him, Matty incarnates potential, not actual, salvation. To be saved humanity must accept but also generate the good, as Matty concludes in his journal: "What good is not breathed into the world by the holy spirit must come down by and through the nature of man." Only in the unlikely event that man chooses no longer to reject but to emulate Christ —

and Matty — will the necessary change of heart take place. Meanwhile, Sim's words seem best to express the dark truth of the human condition: "We're all mad, the whole damned race. We're wrapped in illusions, delusions, confusions about the penetrability of partitions, we're all mad and in solitary confinement."

9

Sentimental Journey:
The Sea Trilogy

Rites of Passage (1980) ends in midocean, its aging ship of the line bound for Australia having got "from the coast of England a little beyond the equator." In the unfinished voyage lay the potential for the great sea trilogy that Golding would complete nearly a decade later: "You could get another couple of volumes about that voyage, if you wanted."[1] Those volumes — *Close Quarters* (1987) and *Fire down Below* (1989) — like the first, trace in the pages of Edmund Fitzhenry Talbot's journal the tortuous progress of the increasingly decrepit old warship. A young man of "boundless ambition" journeying from one world to another "to assist the governor in the administration of one of His Majesty's colonies," Talbot addresses the journal to his godfather, the aristocratic patron whose "kindly hand" has set his "foot on the ladder." Written with all the easy wit and fluid grace expected of an English gentleman coming of age in the period of the Napoleonic wars — "round about 1812 or 1813," says Golding — the journal inevitably chronicles not only Talbot's observations but his initiation. Transition — geographical, historical, psychological — is the subject of nearly every journal entry. Coincident with the ship's abandonment of familiar for unfamiliar waters is the dissolving of eighteenth- into nineteenth-century sensibility and the widening of Talbot's perspective on his fellow voyagers and on himself. A microcosm of the larger world, the ship brings together people from all social classes. Talbot likens it to the biblical ark and Captain Anderson to Noah. On the ship, as in England, class distinctions are scrupulously preserved. Yet even though class boundaries are clearly demarcated on board Golding's "floating theatre," the "varied fabrics of the human tapestry" are necessarily more proximate to one another than they would be on land. The "stench" that nauseates Talbot when he first comes aboard is unnoticed by his servant, Wheeler. What Talbot learns in the course of his matriculation at sea has centrally to do with getting used to the stink of common humanity.

Rites of Passage

"It's a black comedy with relevance to the present situation," says Golding of *Rites of Passage*. Even "more directly than *The Pyramid*," it is "all about class.... It's making some urgent statements about class. Unless we can get rid of it or at least blunt the pyramid or make it a little less monumental, we're done, we're finished, and it had better happen quickly."[2] Talbot's essential decency is marred by the instinctive superciliousness of a young English gentleman insulated by birth, wealth, and education from the great majority of his fellowmen. So axiomatic is his sense of class privilege that he regards the ordinary sailors as scarcely human on the one hand and casually strolls into the forbidden "Sacred Precincts" of the Captain's quarterdeck on the other. That Talbot is nonetheless capable of growth is also fittingly expressed in terms of class. Late in the novel he is able to correct his condescendingly superior attitude toward the admirable Lieutenant Summers, a onetime common sailor who has, incredibly, risen through the ranks. At the same time he revises downward his instinctive approbation of the well-born but scurrilous Lieutenant Deverel. In both cases Talbot's heightened awareness of others — and of himself — arises from that receptivity to experience that permits the evidence of his eyes to override the prejudices of his class. The initiation motif in *Rites of Passage* recalls that of *The Pyramid:* Talbot, like Oliver, matures in accordance with his ability to "blunt the pyramid" of class.

If the title of the novel epitomizes Talbot's rite de passage as well as attendant shipboard rituals, it also reflects a historical period. As historical watershed, the Napoleonic Wars rival World War II, Golding's usual zone of demarcation between two worlds. Perhaps because his own war triggered a critical shift in his consciousness, Golding situates his novels at moments of transition. Although an old order yields most obviously to a new in *The Inheritors,* the effect is characteristically produced by World War II. A before-and-after scenario bisected by the war is invoked at least implicitly in every Golding novel set in the twentieth century. In *Rites of Passage* the eighteenth century dissolves into the nineteenth, neoclassicism into romanticism. This historical and intellectual shift is mirrored in Talbot's "evolution." An eighteenth-century man of reason, he becomes in the course of the voyage a nineteenth-century man of feeling as well. This he characteristically accomplishes by amending another hasty judgment dictated by the very class prejudices that blinded him to the relative worth of Lieutenants Summers and Deverel. Robert James Colley, whose awkward physique, speech, and manners betray the lower-class origin that his religious vocation apparently denies, is for Talbot initially an object of scorn. A parson who, in Talbot's view, "has stepped out of his station without any merit to support the elevation," Colley embodies the folly of violating the social hierarchy. Colley, too, keeps a journal whose rapturous paeans to nature sharply contrast with Talbot's narrower focus on human intercourse. It is chiefly in their divergent styles and sensibilities rather than in the outward events of the voyage that Golding represents the moment of transition between two eras.

Because the events of the voyage as well as Colley's account of them are filtered through Talbot's journal entries, writing becomes not only a means of narration but an end in itself. And because he writes for an aristocratic and sophisticated patron, Talbot must take pains with the form as well as the content of his journal. An inveterately self-conscious narrator, Talbot invokes a pantheon of eighteenth-century writers, perhaps as much to demonstrate his literary acumen as to identify appropriate role models. In any event, he proposes to write more like "lively old Fielding and Smollett" than "sentimental Goldsmith or Richardson," but finds himself echoing Sterne in the brevity and digressiveness of his journal entries and even mimicking the chapter headings — Alpha, Beta, etc. — of *Tristram Shandy.* As an epistolary novel whose "author" is its hero, *Rites of Passage* evokes a historical period not only by adapting one of its conventional forms but by adopting one of its cherished strategies: imitation. And beyond its parody of a legitimate eighteenth-century literary form lies an actual journal — Scawen Blunt's account of a 1797 episode at sea — that greatly inspired *Rites of Passage.* Colley's death — and its probable cause — is prefigured in the fate of Blunt's clergyman who got "abominably drunk" and appeared stark naked among the ship's crew, talking and singing scatologically. So deeply did he feel his disgrace that in "ten days he forced himself to die of contrition." This phenomenon of a willed death was "so horrific that I had to invent human circumstances to make us understand how a man could die of shame."[3] In thus explaining the genesis of *Rites of Passage* Golding pinpoints the thematic centrality of what happens to Colley.

Colley's fall is rooted in class — "the British language," Summers rightly calls it. Captain Anderson, forced to suppress his anger when the socially unassailable Talbot heedlessly enters his private domain, vents his pent-up rage against the defenseless Colley who similarly but innocently blunders into the same forbidden territory. Thus Anderson and Talbot are indirectly implicated in Colley's death, along with the common seamen — abetted by Lieutenants Cumbershum and Deverel — who brutally assault him in the "Crossing the Line" ceremony. Yet without discounting class, sex is the immediate culprit in Colley's fall, as it is so often in Golding's fiction. As Colley himself writes, the ultimate responsibility for the tragedy that overtakes him is his own: "What a man does defiles him, not what is done by others." Colley's brand of self-defilement is sexual: after openly parading drunk and half-naked and pissing against the ship's mast, he performs fellatio on the handsome seaman, Billy Rogers. The parson's descent into the darkness of the ship's hull turns out to be a descent into the darkness of himself. Inspired by "the devil's brew," Colley's immediate reaction to the incident is ecstatic: "Joy! Joy! Joy!" But the euphoria of sexual liberation, conceived in drunkenness, vanishes in sobriety. Self-knowledge liberates Colley only to destroy him. The surfacing of his repressed homosexuality reveals to him the discrepancy between his true nature and that of the "Spiritual Man" he felt himself to be. Colley's suffering may stem from the same hubris that afflicted Jocelin, another man of God, in *The Spire*. Like Jocelin, Colley believes that his calling separates him from ordinary people. Forgiving Lieutenants Cumbershum and Deverel for their part in his equatorial mishaps, he self-consciously imitates Christ: "Go, and sin no more." Although his "disgusting" behavior revealed not so much the monstrous in himself as the double nature all men share, Colley cannot live with the knowledge of his own commonality. Sex and class converge in his despair: in drunkenly violating a sexual taboo, Colley has forfeited the privileged class status accorded the clergy. It is the translation of moral into social disgrace that largely accounts for his willed death. Talbot's conclusion that Colley died from remembering the fellatio incident predictably but accurately exposes its social ramifications: "Forced back toward his own kind...."

That Colley appears in clerical dress — "Those *ornaments* of the Spiritual Man" — when he goes among the crew "to bring them to repentance" illustrates not only his misplaced pride but his incredible naïveté. Far from commanding the automatic respect that he anticipates, Colley's ecclesiastical finery provokes his baiting in the "Crossing the Line" ceremony. His trust in the power of his parson's cloth — and of the religion it represents — evinces a belief in the established social order akin to Talbot's. Significantly, the clothes of his calling are stripped away in the public drunkenness and sexual errancy that reveal him as all too human. Religious symbolism, subverted in the inefficacy of priestly clothing, is burlesqued in the "rites" of Colley's degradation. He is baptized in "filthy water" after being smeared with excrement as part of the "Crossing the Line" ceremony. Subsequently Colley perverts the communion sacrament by performing fellatio on Billy Rogers. And he presumptuously likens his own suffering to Christ's and emulates his "Master" in forgiving his tormentors.

As the vilified, persecuted, and rejected scapegoat Colley superficially resembles Matty of *Darkness Visible*. Like Matty, he embodies religious belief in a notably secular environment; and their spiritual transports are identically expressed in the word *joy*. Yet the blasphemous travesty of baptism and communion suggests that Colley's affinity with Matty is more apparent than real. Matty's joy derives from mystical revelation, Colley's from a bout of drunken and sordid sex. And Colley, unlike Matty, is much concerned with keeping up appearances; when appearances can no longer be preserved Colley despairs of living and dies of shame. His passive and pathetic death is the antithesis of Matty's fiery apotheosis, a betrayal not an affirmation of Christianity. Conceived in despair and deliberately undertaken, Colley's death is tantamount to suicide — the gravest of mortal sins. Matty dies to save a child and redeem a sinner, Colley to save face and to redeem himself from embarrassment. From Colley's death Talbot learns something about the opacity of human motivation and the consequent need for greater tolerance of, if not empathy with, other people. Yet the entire Colley affair is only a single aspect, albeit an important one, of Talbot's rite of passage. Golding himself explodes the temptation to take the parson too seriously: "I think he's a silly ass, Colley. I think he is naive rather than innocent." Implicit in this debunking of Colley is the impossibility of likening him to Christ. Colley's is the fate of a frustrated parvenu not a martyred saint: "I think he is led astray by his own faith in the social pyramid.

The great thing in Colley's life is that he has hitched himself up a little bit in the pyramid beyond his origins. The terrible thing for Colley would be to fall below that, and of course he does, with a crash. And that is the end of him."[4] Talbot's view — that Colley is "clownish" and that his death from a "ridiculous schoolboy trick" is no less farcical than tragic — seems to echo Golding's. To mistake Colley for a tragic hero is to overestimate his role and thus to disrupt the novel's delicate balance. Rereading *Rites of Passage* a few years after its publication, Golding maintained that the book "ought to be viewed much more as an entertainment... I thought a lot of it was just funny. It's a black comedy, of course, but most comedy nowadays is black."[5]

A good deal of the comedy of *Rites of Passage* — black and otherwise — originates in the perceived disparity between action and effect. Colley's overpowering sense of guilt, not to mention his self-willed death, seems vastly disproportionate to his "sin" with Billy Rogers. On a lighter note, Talbot "seduces" Zenobia Brocklebank as books rain down upon them; and an explosion above decks that alarms Zenobia results only in his premature ejaculation, completing the dissolution of passion into farce. Moreover, the tumbling books slyly evoke Golding's strategy for maintaining the serio-comic equilibrium of *Rites of Passage*. In this most "literary" of his novels, Golding multiplies the textual inversions and subversions that mark nearly all of his fiction. Adding to the deliberate artifice (a term more honored than reviled in pre-Romantic literature) of the textual backgrounding is an equally deliberate attempt to reproduce eighteenth-century literary style. What results from this convergence of matter and method emphasizes the ironic distancing already achieved by casting *Rites of Passage* in the form of a diary. Because Talbot's retrospective and self-conscious textualization of events *becomes* the events, they are a step removed from "reality." Talbot wants not so much to transcribe the minutiae of shipboard life as to fashion it into a piece of literature artful enough to amuse his sophisticated patron and, not inciden-

tally, to valorize himself. His many textual references invoke
literary models as they validate his own taste. In an era that
valued tasteful imitation above idiosyncratic originality, Talbot aims not to exceed but to conform to the norms of civilized
discourse. By the time he first confides his intention eventually
to publish his journals, it comes as no surprise.

In addition to the specific writers Talbot mentions and
the epistolary style he employs, a number of oblique references to period texts reanimate the historical moment of
Rites of Passage. Jane Austen's *Pride and Prejudice,* another
novel much concerned with class and manners, may provide in the parvenu clergyman Mr. Collins the original of
Golding's Mr. Colley. Not only the epistolary narrative but
the device of complementary journals in *Rites of Passage*
may reflect *Humphrey Clinker,* Tobias Smollett's eighteenth-
century travel novel. More obscurely, the sexual component
of Colley's shame and the letter to his sister may be suggested
respectively by Samuel Richardson's *Clarissa* and Henry Fielding's *Joseph Andrews.* Yet despite Golding's tactic of evoking
neoclassic sense and sensibility via period texts, the most
pervasive and resonant literary references in *Rites of Passage* derive not from eighteenth- but from nineteenth-century
works. Because the historicity of *Rites of Passage* is less an
end in itself than a means of "making some urgent statements
about class," the novel's universal applicability is suggested
as much by its transcendence as by its imitation of eighteenth
century analogues.[6] Among the many writers Golding invokes
in *Rites of Passage,* three figure most prominently: Samuel
Taylor Coleridge, Herman Melville, and Joseph Conrad. Like
Golding, these nineteenth-century writers famously exploit
sea, ship, and voyage as components of a morally resonant
mise-en-scène.

Two Coleridge poems — "Rime of the Ancient Mariner"
primarily but "Dejection: An Ode" as well — not only illumi-
nate Colley's ordeal and its aftermath but signal the imminent
decline of Enlightenment and the rise of Romantic values.
Although Colley's ostracization and victimization recall the

sufferings of the Ancient Mariner, their divergent fates suggest that Golding's symbolic voyage differs importantly from Coleridge's. Like the Mariner, Colley is filled with universal love: "I am consumed by a great love of all things." And his "Joy! Joy! Joy!" echoes the language of emotional rapture common to both Coleridge poems. But the Mariner's epiphany frees him from guilt and leads to his spiritual rebirth; Colley's merely postpones the onset of guilt (he is, after all, drunk) and leads (given its suicidal overtones) to his spiritual death. If Colley cannot sustain Coleridgean joy, he is nonetheless its sole spokesman in *Rites of Passage*. The revelations in Colley's letter shake Talbot's complacent worldview, an outlook compounded of surface appearance and social prejudice. In acknowledging Colley as a complex human being rather than a social cipher, Talbot is shamed into an implicit confession of his own moral blindness. His conclusion — "Life is a formless business.... Literature is much amiss in forcing a form on it" — constitutes, among other things, a devastating self-indictment that conceivably invalidates the entire journal-keeping enterprise. Talbot, who once tacitly approved of Zenobia's mocking rendition of the "Rime of the Ancient Mariner" refrain and poked fun at the albatross legend, ends by invoking Coleridge's verse as Colley's epitaph: "All, all alone." This recourse to Coleridge at the end of *Rites of Passage* falls well short of embracing Romantic sensibility. Yet Talbot's belated awakening marks the emergence, however provisional and unformulated, of a deeper and more comprehensive outlook.

While its fundamental shift in sensibility is conceived primarily in Coleridgean terms, Melville's *Billy Budd* and Conrad's *Heart of Darkness* also spotlight key aspects of *Rites of Passage*. Melville's eponymous hero is, like Golding's Billy Rogers, a handsome foretopman who figures prominently in a shipboard tragedy. There, however, the resemblance ends. Billy Rogers "is diametrically opposite" to "the other Billy," avers Golding, acknowledging that his character is a deliberate inversion of Melville's.[7] To locate in Rogers the corruption

148   William Golding

that destroys Colley is to recall its absolute antithesis in the
saintly innocence of Budd. Budd incarnates innocence destroyed, Rogers the destroyer of innocence. It may be that
Golding evokes Billy Budd to exemplify the Christian martyrdom parodied in Colley's death. This ironic contrast between
the real tragedy of Billy Budd and the mock tragedy sparked
by Billy Rogers apparently reflects Golding's estimate of "poor
old Colley" who "goes through a rite of passage" but "fails
to make the grade."[8] Aside from inspiring Golding's anti-Billy
Budd, Melville's story may contribute to the shipboard atmosphere of *Rites of Passage*. Golding's ship, like Melville's, is a
microcosm of society at large, its oppressively autocratic rule
similarly rationalized by an ongoing war. Aboard both ships,
godlike captains determine the fate of essentially innocent
victims: Captain Vere convenes the drumhead court-martial
less to ascertain Budd's guilt than to sanction his execution;
and Captain Anderson effectively, albeit unknowingly, precipitates Colley's death by deliberately ignoring his persecution
by the crew. Still, the net result of appropriating Melville's
text is to spotlight the difference between the tragedy of
Billy Budd and the black comedy of *Rites of Passage*. Golding achieves his effect chiefly by splintering Billy Budd into
Rogers and Colley. Rogers inherits Budd's shipboard station
and handsome features, Colley his innocence and destiny. But
Rogers's outward beauty masks his inward depravity; and
Colley's innocence and destiny are treated ambivalently. Golding's transmutation of Melville's cosmic tragedy into social
comedy is nowhere more apparent than in the key confrontation between Rogers and Colley, the debased halves of Billy
Budd. That the act of fellatio is arguably the central event
of *Rites of Passage* — its only competitor is Colley's death
that it, of course, precipitates — reflects Golding's seriocomic
intentions.

Echoing and permuting the "Rime of the Ancient Mariner"
and *Billy Budd*, Golding sharpens the focus — stylistic, historical, thematic — of *Rites of Passage*. One last text — Conrad's
Heart of Darkness — empowers the denouement. To invoke

Heart of Darkness as a paradigm is unsurprising: "The use of Conrad as posing a class and moral problem for the civilised European recurs throughout Golding's fiction."[9] After Colley dies, the letter he had written to his sister in England is discovered by Talbot who determines not to forward it but to replace it with one of his own that "contains everything but a shred of truth." At the same time he decides "to increase the small store of money that will be returned to her." Like Marlow, the narrator of *Heart of Darkness* who similarly suppressed Kurtz's story, Talbot elects to lie in the name of mercy and in the service of a greater truth: that man is finally unknowable. What "truth" Colley's sister and Kurtz's fiancée would have learned from the withheld information is no more or less contingent than the "fiction" that displaces it. Like Kurtz, Colley confronted his own heart of darkness with devastating consequences. And while Colley's latent homosexuality is hardly tantamount to Kurtz's overt savagery, Talbot's decision to lie is as moral an action as Marlow's. Marlow's trip up the Congo throws "a kind of light" all about him and into his thought. Talbot's is equally a voyage of discovery, climaxing like Marlow's in an encounter with another that proves also to be an encounter with the self. It may be that Marlow exemplifies what Talbot is in the process of becoming: *Homo moralis*. An older and wiser man than Talbot, Marlow incarnates the emotional receptivity essential for moral growth. Colley's letter reveals to Talbot the hidden depths of human experience his own account of the voyage so glaringly omitted. In confronting his own superficiality, Talbot transcends it and takes his first halting step toward the palace of wisdom.

Close Quarters

The title of this second book of Edmund Talbot's travels derives from the increasingly claustrophobic shipboard conditions he remarks on in the final words of *Rites of Passage*: "With lack of sleep and too much understanding I grow a little crazy, I think, like all men at sea who live too close to each other and too close thereby to all that is monstrous under the sun and moon." Yet *Close Quarters* seems designed not so much to reveal the sinister implications of *monstrous* as to certify Golding's seriocomic intentions. That the novel — and the trilogy — is essentially comedy flecked with tragedy rather than vice versa grows ever more apparent in the course of *Close Quarters* and inescapable in *Fire down Below,* its sequel. Thus it eventually turns out that *Rites of Passage,* far from invoking the mise-en-scène of mounting disaster, had actually incorporated in Colley's story and its aftermath the most serious and potentially tragic elements of the entire trilogy. Nothing Talbot learns in *Close Quarters* effects his rite of passage so indispensably as what he learned about and from Colley. Indeed Colley's presiding spirit is repeatedly re-invoked at those moments when Talbot confronts himself as he had first learned to do in *Rites of Passage.* At key points in *Close Quarters* Talbot even appropriates elements of Colley's identity. These successive stages in the transformation of consciousness that largely constitutes Talbot's rite of passage are suffused by Colley's symbolic presence. When Talbot falls in love with Marion Chumley at first sight of her aboard the frigate *Alcyone,* he reenacts the emotional raptures Billy Rogers inspired in Colley. Formerly the avatar of eighteenth-century decorum, Talbot becomes "an advocate of impropriety," behaving in an "impossibly familiar" manner towards Miss Chumley in public. With each succeeding demonstration of the emotional spontaneity that he once contemptuously derided in Colley, Talbot sheds a layer of his former self and inches toward becoming the sort of man he had previously reviled. Golding's way of dramatizing the changes in Talbot is thus to involve him in the sort of romantic scenario that rivals Colley's in its incongruity. So crazed with love does Talbot become — he has, incidentally, suffered a concussion just prior to being fatally smitten by Miss Chumley's charms — that he initiates the madcap scheme of transferring his inamorata to his own hopefully surrendered cabin. Significantly, he moves himself into the hutch where Colley died, thereby spotlighting his growing identification with the dead parson. Although Summers saves Talbot from the total abandonment of joining Miss Chumley aboard the *Alcyone* bound for India by shutting him up in his new cabin (there to suffer the same "humiliations of delirium" once endured by Colley) it is clear that the febrile lover of *Close Quarters* bears little resemblance to the cool tumbler of Zenobia Brocklebank in *Rites of Passage*. Regarding himself in a mirror, the recovering Talbot sees a "face...so thin as to be positively bony" — a face, in short, like Colley's. In contemplating the impossibility that "a skull should shrink," Talbot confronts beneath the skin of human disparity the skull of human commonality.

The primary effect of this reality-versus-appearance motif is to question the validity of perceptions, particularly Talbot's. Whether to explode the smug doctrine of first impressions underlying Talbot's pigeonholing of passengers and crew in *Rites of Passage* or simply because the second novel of a trilogy invariably marks time, actions tend to dissolve in *Close Quarters*. Those surrounding Talbot's abortive love affair seem particularly to epitomize a strategy of authorial subversion. Thus Talbot's display of bravery in volunteering to join Lieutenant Deverel's boarding party comes to nothing when *Alcyone*, mistakenly identified as an enemy warship, turns out to be a British frigate. Paralleling the false urgency of night alarms and battle stations in its near-comic futility is Talbot's feverish pursuit of Miss Chumley. Evoked only to be denied, war and love are similarly drained of their narrative potential, sacrificed to the exigencies of theme. That theme is, above all, metamorphic: to represent the incremental changes in Talbot by subverting the stability not only of actions but of actors. Thus the glamorous Zenobia Brocklebank is revealed as ghastly, "Gentleman" Jack Deverel as a drunkard. Golding's reductive methodology extends even to such matters as the name *Alcyone*, subverting its associations with *halcyon* and, more obscurely, with the kingfisher. A bird whose legendary power to calm the sea is hardly relevant to the becalmed condition of Captain Anderson's ship, the kingfisher — harbinger of redemption in *The Spire* — promises nothing in *Close Quarters*. The novel's essential inconclusiveness is already apparent at its outset when Talbot's "expectation that some material fit for permanence would appear — but nothing" predicts its ensuing course. Similarly, Talbot's search for a "hero for my new journal, a new heroine, a new villain and some comic relief to ameliorate my deep, deep boredom" is largely futile. No hero materializes; the putative heroine, Miss Chumley, and the potential villain, Lieutenant Deverel, sail away on *Alcyone*; and the comic relief is sporadic at best.

The frustrating search for matter is complemented by the no less frustrating struggle with form. Both are attributable to a single factor: the absence of Colley. Even the suicide of Wheeler, who blows his brains out in Talbot's cabin, serves primarily to recall Colley, who died in the same place. Yet Wheeler's suicide in the final chapter is only the latest and most striking of the many evocations of Colley that pervade the entire novel. The dead parson is invariably recalled at those moments when Talbot despairs of finding the right words to express himself. Emerging from the delirium induced by concussion and exacerbated by the "loss" of Miss Chumley, Talbot acknowledges the probability "that without Colley's natural ability in the art of description there is no way in which I can convey the confusion of what happened." Later, leafing through his journal, Talbot laments its deficiencies: "But this one lacked the accidental shape of narration which Colley and fate had forced on the other volume!" To enliven his account of the voyage, Talbot again invokes Colley's descriptive powers: "Colley said much of colour! I must remember the colour of things." Finally, in his *postscriptum,* Talbot reveals most specifically and most fully how much his own writing owes to Colley's. Rereading "book one," Talbot finds "it had gained a great deal by the inclusion of Colley's affecting if unfinished letter.... There was a touch of genius in his vivid and fluent use of his native tongue: whereas 'book two' must rely on my own unaided efforts." The forthcoming "book three" must depend upon "the strangeness and hazard of the events" to "compensate for the plainness of the writing," since "I cannot pretend to Colley's talent."

Although it is for his writing that Colley is chiefly remembered, the letter whose presence animated *Rites of Passage* and whose absence enfeebled *Close Quarters* is less crucial for its style than for its revelation of Colley and its impact on Talbot. Not the imitation of a style but the appropriation of the outlook that begets it marks a watershed in Talbot's rite of passage. Via the medium of Colley's letter Talbot is imbued with the Coleridgean universal love that suffuses it. The Talbot who repeatedly and unabashedly dissolves into tears in *Close Quarters* is a far cry from the aloof and distant "Lord Talbot," the soubriquet his hauteur earned in *Rites of Passage*. Shortly after suffering blows to the head and moving into Colley's former cabin — the physical symptoms of forthcoming metaphysical change — Talbot joins the gala entertainment attended by the people of the two ships. There he is transported by Mrs. East's song that somehow evokes "the boatswain's call" that "haunted" him "after the funeral of poor Colley." For Talbot, the simple song opens "new palaces of feeling," and triggers an epiphany of self-awareness: "Those tears which I had been able to restrain at my introduction to a new life now fell...they were tears of *understanding!*" That Mrs. East's song strikes a sympathetic chord in Talbot testifies to his newfound capacity for heartfelt response to his fellow human beings. It is this new Talbot, helplessly fainting after Wheeler's suicide, whose transformation inspires and validates Miss Granham's judgment: "Poor boy. He has far more sensibility than he knows."

Fire down Below

Talbot's metamorphosis into a man of feeling — a character type repeatedly invoked and often idealized in the fiction of his day — is triumphantly concluded in *Fire down Below*.

So aware of his shortcomings and eager to remedy them has Talbot become that he seizes upon any evidence of beneficent change. A simple change from a gentleman's clothes to a common seaman's symbolizes for Talbot "my own escape from a certain unnatural stiffness and even *hauteur*." As if to certify the new identity conferred by the change of clothes, he acts the midshipman, joining Summers to "stand a watch." On one of their watches, Summers jokingly mimics Talbot's stiffly formal description of a suitable young lady, eliciting the preternatural sensitivity that characterizes the man of feeling: "It is certainly how I used to think in my nasty calculating way." The refashioned Talbot's habit of self-deprecation — symptomatic of the "sadness of self-knowledge" — transcends mundane details of speech and manner. "You could have saved us," he cries out in his sleep, echoing the imagined accusations of the dead Colley and Wheeler. More anguish arises from his conviction that he has hastened Mr. Prettiman's death. That he buries Prettiman prematurely — the gravely ill man eventually recovers — evidences Talbot's sometimes unseemly contrition. His endless mea culpas threaten to make a virtue of self-castigation, converting it into a mode of self-congratulation. Excessive remorse so features his relationship with Summers that their growing friendship seems comically predicated on Talbot's incessant apologies. Whether or not he is constantly on the lookout for occasions to demonstrate his hard-won sensibility, Talbot verges toward the unreflective feeling that is arguably no better than his former unfeeling reflection.

Because of the importance of the friendship motif — Talbot frequently invokes the Glaucus and Diomede story in the *Iliad* — what passes between Talbot and Summers constitutes much of the narrative of *Fire down Below*. Especially during the hours of their shared watch, the two come to form a mutual admiration society chiefly devoted to reassuring each other. Summers assures Talbot of Miss Chumley's love; and Talbot repeats his offer to do what he can to advance Summers's career. More important, Talbot sides openly with Summers whose opposition to Lieutenant Benét's radical schemes for increasing the ship's speed has earned Captain Anderson's displeasure. But just as his excess of reason once betrayed him into undervaluing people, notably Colley, Talbot's new excess of feeling leads him to valorize Summers at the expense of the more clever and ingenious, albeit flashy, Benét. It is, after all, Benét's fire down below — the welding operation that rights the mast — that speeds the nearly becalmed "superannuated hulk" on its way and conceivably saves the lives of all aboard. Talbot's steadfast loyalty to Summers is laudable in its demonstration of a capacity for human warmth that had hitherto flared only sporadically. Yet it is misguided in its willing misinterpretation of the actions and motives of others in the name of friendship. A second important shipboard relationship — that with the Prettimans — is required to effect the stabilization of Talbot's character that marks the successfully completed rite of passage.

Called upon by the apparently dying Mr. Prettiman to witness his will and his marriage to Miss Granham, Talbot is initially contemptuous of them and the prospect of their "furtive, middle-aged sexual congress." Soon, however, he comes to respect their courage and resolution and, as Prettiman begins to recover, Talbot and the couple engage in a series of conversations that comprise the philosophical core of *Fire down Below* and raise his moral consciousness. The first tête-à-tête between Talbot and Prettiman reveals their mutual taste for Pindar whose ode beginning "Gray hairs flourish even among young men" Talbot quotes. To Prettiman, Talbot's familiarity with Greek indicates "some inkling of a wider view," a conclusion supported by the specific words of the quoted passage. Still, Prettiman's hectoring tone miffs Talbot who starts to edge away from an exchange that "was in the very vein of Parson Colley." In the context of their conversation, which Prettiman begs Talbot to continue, the reference to Colley is significant. For Prettiman is an older and wiser version of Colley whose role it is to advance in Talbot the process of education that Colley began. Just as Colley's words affected Talbot's heart, transforming his private outlook, so

Prettiman's affect his mind, transforming his public outlook. Goaded by Prettiman, Talbot discovers the "impossible" — that despite his own classical education, he "had never examined an idea before." Listening to the older man, a political idealist who dreams of founding an Eldorado in Australia, Talbot for the first time in his life questions the "established order," which Prettiman describes as "sick." What Prettiman transmits to Talbot — a "feeling" that "the universe was great and glorious" — hauntingly echoes the lesson of Colley. So "irradiated" is he "by the nature" of the Prettimans that Talbot momentarily throws off his "upbringing" to "stand naked, defenceless, but free!"

That he cannot long maintain the posture of existential freedom invoked by the idealistic Prettimans does no discredit to Talbot who, unable to "elevate" himself "to see Mr. Prettiman's Good, nor his Absolute," nonetheless remains "alive" to the "transcendent beauty" of the Creation. Moreover, although he cannot follow the Prettimans who urge him to "come too," he has achieved a goodly measure of their love for "fire down below here — sparks of the Absolute:" Prettiman's rapturous definition of common humanity. Talbot remains "after all a political animal with my spark...well hidden." Still, his resolve to "exercise power" for the common good, even couched in the rhetoric of English chauvinism that equates "the benefit of the world" with "the betterment of my country," represents a quantum motivational leap for a man who once regarded power solely as a corridor to self-advancement.

After he assimilates — and vows to apply — the altruistic imperative epitomized and enjoined by the Prettimans, Talbot's personal rite of passage effectively ends. Not so the larger trial of the battered ship that must survive a close encounter with a mountainous iceberg that turns out to be Antarctica. That the ship does survive the sort of mandatory ordeal sea stories thrive on, finally to land safely in Australia, comes as no surprise in light of the survival of Talbot's journals. Ashore, Mrs. Prettiman cautions Talbot not to "refine upon" the "nature" of the voyage: "It was not an Odyssey. It is no type, emblem, metaphor of the human condition" but a "series of events." And to his melodramatic fear that "there has been death in my hands," she characteristically replies, "Stuff and nonsense." Mrs. Prettiman's words, intended to dispel the lingering vestiges of portentousness — and pretentiousness — about Talbot, also recall Golding's refusal to call *Rites of Passage* a tragedy. That the entire sea trilogy embodies the "black comedy" Golding attributed to the first volume is clarified in the voyage's aftermath. On land, the snail's pace of the nearly year-long ordeal at sea yields to an almost frenetic succession of scenes whose arbitrary nature, comic in itself, is designed to effect comic closure. Serious, even grave, events are drained of their tragic potential by their rapid occurrence and fleeting consequence. "My future fell in ruins," cries Talbot at news of his godfather's sudden death. Several pages later Summers is blown up and Talbot grievously injured. Yet no sooner is Talbot reduced to unaccommodated man than a series of sudden reversals cancels impending tragedy. First a deus ex machina worthy of Golding's admired Greek drama appears in the form of *Alcyone* with Miss Chumley aboard. Then a much older Talbot, now a distinguished member of Parliament by virtue of election in absentia — another deus ex machina — to his late godfather's rotten borough, reminisces about postvoyage events highlighted by his marriage to "the most beautiful lady in the world!"

Talbot prefaces the account of his miraculous good fortune by invoking "Fielding and Smollett, to say nothing of the moderns, Miss Austen, for example, who feel that despite all the evidence from the daily life around them, a story to be veridical should have a happy ending." His is a "fairy story," Talbot admits just prior to telling how he sighted the "crowned kingfisher" — now converted from an ironic into an actual emblem of redemption — of the *Alcyone*. And, far from having ended with Miss Chumley's arrival, the "fairy tale was about to begin" with the news of his election to Parliament: "Beat that, Goldsmith! Emulate me, Miss Austen, if you are able!" In his exultant literary allusions, Talbot not only aligns the governing aesthetic of his famous contemporaries with his own but provides a likely reading of the sea trilogy. Like the many fictional eighteenth- and nineteenth-century rites of passage it recalls, Talbot's is ultimately a sentimental journey whose mandatory happy ending is validated by the triumphant, if fortuitous, completion of a mostly sentimental education: transformed into a man of feeling, he conforms to the masculine ideal in the literature that he invokes and Golding emulates.

10

Writing and Its Discontents:
The Paper Men

Midway through *Rites of Passage* Edmund Talbot, glanc-
ing sardonically at the goings-on aboard Golding's ship of
fools, imagines himself in a play. "Is it," he muses more face-
tiously than seriously, "a farce or a tragedy?" Invoking ancient
Greek, and his own neoclassic, guidelines, Talbot assumes that
tragedy depends on the dignity of the protagonist. To "fall
greatly" the protagonist must himself be great — an attribute
notably lacking in Colley. "A farce then," concludes Talbot,
"for the man appears now a sort of Punchinello. His fall is in
social terms." Talbot's judgment, amplified in Golding's assertion that *Rites of Passage* is a "black comedy," is equally valid
for *The Paper Men* (1984) and its protagonist, Wilfred Barclay. Not only does Talbot (and Golding) sound a cautionary
note to those critics who take Colley's death as evidence of
high tragedy; he also anticipates a similarly flawed reading of
The Paper Men based on Barclay's violent end. The immediate
successor to *Rites of Passage* and Golding's first post-Nobel
Prize novel, *The Paper Men* evokes the pitfalls of fame in the
pratfalls of its writer-hero. Like the sea trilogy, *The Paper Men*
features a writer writing; what is written — Talbot's journals,
Barclay's autobiography — purports to be the novel Golding
wrote. Barclay envisions his work in progress as a farce, himself as a farceur. As he stalks the badger he imagines to be
rifling his dustbin in the novel's opening episode, clutching
an ancient air gun in one hand and a torch in the other and

lacking a third hand to hold up his slipping pajama trousers, Barclay extrapolates from the ludicrous situation a recurring motif: "I recognized uneasily the hand of what I sometimes thought to be my personal nemesis, the spirit of farce." When the culprit in the dustbin turns out to be not a badger but Professor Rick L. Tucker rummaging for revealing scraps of paper, Barclay's "spirit of farce" seems already to be presiding over *The Paper Men.* Just prior to its closure, Barclay summarizes the novel as successive reenactments of his confrontation with Rick at the dustbin: "It's a fair record of the various times the clown's trousers fell down." A self-confessed clown starring in an admitted farce, Barclay can record but never completely transcend the genre he — and Golding — invokes.

To call *The Paper Men* a farce is not to deny its serious subtext. Like Samuel Beckett's *Waiting for Godot,* to which it has been compared, *The Paper Men* abstracts from the farcical symbiosis of its central characters truths relevant to the general human condition.[1] Play and novel alike portray an absurd modernity of spiritual emptiness and debased human relationships. Yet God, futilely awaited by Beckett's odd couple and belatedly welcomed by Barclay, suffuses both works. Eschatological implications lend to the apparently trivial actions of *Waiting for Godot* and *The Paper Men* whatever value they possess. Farce and eschatology converge near the end of *The Paper Men* in Barclay's fancied stigmata a vicar snidely reminds him is most likely to belong to a thief. The seriocomic moment recalls Vladimir's words on the same topic in *Waiting for Godot:* "One of the thieves was saved. It's a reasonable percentage." While Barclay's ultimate fate is uncertain, the salvation or damnation terminology of its evocation produces a literary "genre" reminiscent of *Waiting for Godot:* eschatological farce. Not that the form marks a radical departure for Golding. *Free Fall* threaded elements of farce (e.g., mistaking a rag for a severed penis) into a similar first-person narrative of an artist whose past sins threaten to damn him. And in *Pincher Martin,* arguably Golding's most eschatological novel, another artist successively impersonates tragic heroes, unaware or unwilling to admit that his frantic role playing smacks more of farce than of tragedy. So definitive is Martin's self-aggrandizing habit that it survives symbolically even in death; no Golding protagonist wears his ego more flagrantly on his sleeve. Because the all-consuming ego symptomizes human sinfulness for Golding, Wilfred Barclay, Martin-like in his self-centeredness, stands indicted. What saves him from moral twinship with Martin — Golding's consummately evil character — may be Barclay's sense of farce. That he sees himself as the clown whose pants keep endlessly falling down dilutes the sinister potential of his admittedly self-serving actions. Even at his most reprehensible Barclay characteristically provokes farce rather than tragedy.

Near the end of *Rites of Passage* Talbot suspects that no literary form can capture life's formlessness. Doubts about writing multiply in *The Paper Men* whose title suggests the insubstantiality of its antagonists. Paper men enmeshed in a paper chase, Barclay and Tucker are players in a game of trivial pursuit that all but mandates farcical treatment. Barclay, a popular but lightweight English novelist living off his royalties, and Tucker, an American academic poseur studying Barclay's relative clauses and hoping to write the official biography, parody literary stereotypes. Barclay dismisses both himself and his bête noire as men who "knew about paper, that was all." Assistant Professor Rick L. Tucker of the University of Astrakhan, Nebraska, wears a pullover inscribed OLE ASHCAN. His lovely but vacuous wife, Mary Lou, majored in flower arranging and bibliography at the same university. Barclay's curmudgeonly reclusiveness and fanciful forwarding addresses (Morocco, Iceland); Tucker's Boy Scout eagerness and doglike obsequiousness; Mary Lou's limpid ethereality and wide-eyed ingenuousness — all are comically exaggerated in the service of farce. At the beginning of chapter 2 Barclay, having shot Tucker for a badger and witnessed Liz's marriage-destroying discovery of a compromising letter from a former mistress, already suspects farce at work: "the corner of a pattern that was to prove itself universal." The remainder of *The*

Paper Men flows from Barclay's need as a writer to select and to interpret, perhaps even to invent, material that will emblazon the farcical pattern he has perceived.

Two literary topoi — the quest plot and the bond plot — are absurdly reconfigured in *The Paper Men*. The quest is potentially trivialized by its protagonists — Barclay and Tucker are hardly Odysseus and Telemachus — as well as by its object — paper. Yet in Henry James's *The Aspern Papers* the paper chase is anything but trivial: "A moral fable for historians and biographers" is how Leon Edel, James's biographer, describes it. For James, the "interest would be in some price that the man has to pay . . . for he really would give almost anything."[2] Golding deliberately cancels this interest by making Tucker a man who would do not *almost* anything but anything at all to become Barclay's official biographer. Lying about academic credentials, rooting through dustbins, playing dog at Barclay's command, even offering Mary Lou as sexual bait — Tucker stops at nothing. In the sense that he, too, cares only about paper, Tucker is Barclay's alter ego. Equally amoral, pursuer and pursued combine to subvert the conventional moral issues of the quest. Even Barclay's refusal to exploit Mary Lou is less the product of moral rectitude than of "humiliation and sheer unalloyed rage. To know myself accepted, endured not even as in honest whoredom, for money, but for *paper!*" In their single-minded dedication to paper Barclay and Tucker recall another James tale, "The Lesson of the Master," where the art-versus-life conundrum is invoked as a red herring. James's point is not that art and life are mutually exclusive but that they are necessarily complementary. To compartmentalize art as a sacred calling that exempts its acolytes from quotidian life is to dehumanize the artist and to devalue his enterprise. "The Lesson of the Master" cautions against the subversion of human values by the paper ideology of a Barclay or a Tucker.

The bond plot not only intersects with the quest plot but illuminates it. In Golding's version of the unholy pact between Marlowe's Dr. Faustus and Mephistopheles, Tucker has been granted seven years by the mysterious billionaire, Halliday, to write Barclay's biography. Tucker buys time by relinquishing Mary Lou to Halliday, a "collector" of young and beautiful women. Mary Lou is reduced to currency, her value determined solely by the paper her sale can buy. The selling of Mary Lou to Halliday — "the old devil," Barclay calls him — is a more desperate and sinister version of the abortive offer to Barclay. Tantamount to Faustus's surrender of his soul to the Devil, Tucker's sellout recalls Golding's familiar habit of representing human sinfulness in sexual exploitation. Thus Tucker plays Faustus to Halliday's Devil only after attempting to play Mephistopheles to Barclay's Faustus. Not surprisingly, Barclay, the consummate paper man, recognizes the Marlowe scenario: "Helen — I mean, Mary Lou — " he cries, slipping momentarily into the role of Faustus dazzled by Helen of Troy. And Barclay even quotes Marlowe's Mephistopheles — "Why, this is Hell, nor am I out of it" — unconsciously anticipating still another juggling of the *Dr. Faustus* roles. Midway through *The Paper Men* the pursuer becomes the pursued, the tempter the tempted. Barclay stops running, "no longer wanting to avoid Rick but rather having a definite need of him to complete things." Their apparently indispensable symbiosis is fittingly reinstated at the same hotel in the Swiss Alps where Barclay had earlier refused to dub Rick his official biographer. Now he tempts Tucker with his signature much as his would-be biographer once tempted him with Mary Lou.

It is Barclay's peripeteia in an Italian cathedral that triggers his decision to meet again with Tucker. Face-to-face with a solid silver statue of Christ, Barclay "knew in one destroying instant that all my adult life I had believed in God and this knowledge was a vision of God . . . I knew my maker and I fell down." At first glance Barclay's undeniably genuine religious epiphany is as unbelievable as it is unforeseen. A cultivator of "universal indifference" who, "on the edge of sixty years old," had "reduced" himself "to what would think least and feel least," Barclay sees himself as nothing but "eyes and appetite." Yet he may always have been, in spite of himself, a seeker after God. If the second half of *The Paper Men* "is con-

cerned with Barclay's flight not from Tucker but from God,"
and the visionary moment in the cathedral is "Barclay's encounter with the God he has been fleeing from," it seems
reasonable to conclude that God has all along lurked at the
fringes of Barclay's consciousness.[3] By the time he returns to
Rome, Barclay regards Halliday not Tucker as the pursuer.
"Clearly more dangerous than Rick," the inscrutable billionaire is missing from *Who's Who in America*, where Barclay
thought to find him. Suddenly Halliday (Holy Day?) materializes on a church roof, patently the "old devil" no longer and,
conceivably, God. It is this symbolic metamorphosis of Halliday — "he must be behind the whole operation," concludes
Barclay — that raises the stakes of the paper chase. The vision of Halliday surmounting the church flows into Barclay's
dream of the Spanish steps, curved like a musical instrument
and bathed in radiance. Young people, making music on the
steps, lead Barclay through a narrow door to a "dark calm sea
beyond it" teeming with singing creatures. Waking, he "wept
and went on weeping...the pain and the strain gone...and
no more need to run."

With the pileup of religious signifiers that begins in earnest
before the statue of Christ and culminates in the dream
of celestial harmony, Barclay's redemption seems imminent.
Formerly a man who went to church for stained glass and re-
laxation after a drink and who refused to credit Padre Pio's
apparent stigmata, Barclay, beset first by a consuming sense
of guilt — "I am sin" — and then by stigmata of his own, is
poised to trade clowning for belief, damnation for salvation.
Yet even as he confronts the silver Christ Barclay questions
its identity: "Perhaps they had inherited it in these parts and
just changed the name and it was Pluto, the god of the Underworld, Hades, striding forward." Christ or Pluto, the statue
fills Barclay with a "dreadful luminescence," which obliterates
everything but the truth of his spiritual state: "predestined and
damned, the divine justice without mercy." From his spiritual
torpor Barclay awakens not to a vision of heavenly bliss but
of the "eternal fix." The statue was, after all, "a steel Hades,"

he decides, and "I had been created by that ghastly intolerance in its own image." It appears that "Barclay has found his maker but not his saviour or redeemer, rather his judge, executioner and torturer."[4] Still, he has passed beyond unbelief to the surety that "we did not . . . invent ourselves"; even to classify himself as one of the "predestinate damned" is to invoke an eschatological vocabulary that the old Barclay would have derided.

In consigning himself to hell Barclay not only rushes to judgment but preempts the role of God. Ever the egoist, he discovers in the statue a God fashioned in his own image and sharing his rigidity and intolerance. What Barclay has made of his life is revealed in a chance encounter with Johnny St. John, a campily homosexual literary friend, on the Greek island of Lesbos. An incisive analyst despite his outré demeanor, St. John evokes a scarifying image that will linger hauntingly in Barclay's memory: "You . . . have spent your life inventing a skeleton on the outside . . . get rid of the armour, the exoskeleton, the carapace, before it's too late." Encased in his protective sheath — "Like crabs and lobsters" — Barclay resembles another hard-shelled egoist — Pincher Martin — who was finally reduced to a pair of lobster claws. Barclay's shell, like Martin's, isolates him from human fellowship; both men are loners whose sporadic interpersonal relationships are predictably hostile. And like Martin's, Barclay's remembrances of things past are invariably debasing: "There was not a single absurd, humiliating or quasi-criminal act in my life that did not come back to sting and burn me." His bad faith dealings with women; his theft of the one good idea *"hidden in Prescott's awful manuscript"* for his fourth novel; his hit-and-run collision with an Indian who "walked right across the road into my headlights" in South America typify the conduct of his life. The alienating shell absolves Barclay not only from human commitment but from the moral imperatives that it rightly engenders. It confers a freedom that consists chiefly of running away: from "some enormous oaf" as a youthful rugby player; from the failed marriage with

Liz; from Tucker; and from Halliday/God. And he is preparing to run again in the novel's last chapter, this despite his recognition after the cathedral scene: "Freedom should carry a government health warning like cancer sticks!" Barclay's apparently sardonic claim to be "a true Christian child of the twentieth century" is not entirely facetious. Together with his meaningless freedom — symbolized by endlessly traversing the anonymous concrete of countless superhighways, his facile and empty work, and his deranged personal relationships — the claim invokes a frightening typicality. To a greater or lesser degree Barclay's are the tracts of other artist protagonists — Pincher Martin, Sammy Mountjoy, Oliver — who inhabit Golding's contemporary wastelands. And like *Pincher Martin, Free Fall,* and *The Pyramid, The Paper Men* savages the sinful and godless modern world it depicts.

With Tucker, Barclay simply reenacts the central motif — deception — and its invariable expression — flight — of his life. In Tucker, however, he encounters another paper man, one whose motives and actions are as unworthy as his own. Tucker lies about his academic credentials, about his "friendship" with John Crowe Ransom, and, at a scholarly convention, about his "deep personal relationship" with Barclay. The stealthy dustbin raid that inadvertently destroys Barclay's marriage; the intrusive picture taking and surreptitious conversation taping; the willingness to sacrifice Mary Lou; the phony Alpine life-saving stunt contrived to incur a sense of obligation in Barclay — all symptomize Tucker's intent to purchase paper at any price. His parasitic desire to appropriate Barclay's life is matched, however, by Barclay's determination to prevent the "sedulous search into a past raw with unforgiving memories." That neither Barclay's life and work nor Tucker's prospective biography warrant the intellectual and emotional investment of their mutually destructive pas de deux is obvious early on. Indeed the rubbish Tucker so assiduously sifts in Barclay's dustbin is as fitting a metaphor as any for the paper sought by the professor and withheld by the writer. It is to Barclay's credit that he acknowledges not only the farcicality of the paper chase per se but also the mediocrity of his own art and of the scholarship it promises to inspire. Thus Tucker "could find no one better, no one behind whom the pseudo-scholars were not queuing up in our dreadful explosion of reconstituted rubbish."

It may be, however, that the farce of the paper chase is the linchpin of the potentially salvational scenario of *The Paper Men*. For it is Barclay's comical flight — a microcosm of the farce of his life — from his real and imagined pursuers that leads him inexorably to his spiritual rendezvous with the silver statue. *"Mea maxima culpa"* are the first words he utters when he regains consciousness after being "struck down in the cathedral." No guarantor of redemption, Barclay's act of contrition is at least its necessary precursor. Unfortunately, the old Barclay persists even as the new Barclay struggles to be born. Moral ambivalence is most evident in his resumed relationship with Tucker. On the one hand Barclay promises permission for his biography, on the other he uses the promise as bait to humiliate Tucker, making him play dog and lap wine up from a saucer, and insisting that the biography reveal his exploitation of Mary Lou. Just as he seems bent on living up to his own billing — the "predestinate damned" — by pushing his victim to the breaking point, Barclay experiences the epiphany of the Spanish Steps. Like *Free Fall*'s Sammy Mountjoy, he first perceives the inner depravity of man, then receives an ameliorating vision of universal harmony. Both men undergo a spiritual conversion whose final outcome is unresolved. Throughout the remainder of *The Paper Men* Barclay continues to eddy between his newfound assent and his habitual denial. If the fearful encounter with the silver Christ/Pluto was meant to demonstrate God's wrath, then the celestial sound and light show on the Spanish Steps is meant to reveal His mercy. Like the appearance of the spectral seaman to an even more recalcitrant Pincher Martin, the vision seems to be God's way of offering Barclay an eleventh-hour reprieve from damnation. Unlike Martin who adamantly — and impossibly — refuses to abandon the shell of his ego, Barclay sees the light. His change of heart is symbolized in the vision's transformation of the human trash that "littered" the Spanish Steps into the "creatures of the sea that sang." And the visionary passage ends with the awestruck Barclay, uncharacteristically speechless, implicitly acknowledging the limits of his art: "For the singing and the song I have no words at all." Irradiated for the first time in his life with happiness, he accepts the mortality that Pincher Martin struggles endlessly and in vain to evade: "I knew that the way I was going, towards death, was the way everybody goes, that it was — healthy and right and *consonant.*" Yet because these consolatory words about death are addressed to the dying Liz, they curdle into galling irony. Equally ironic is his timing: ravaged by the cancer that will shortly kill her, Liz is too far gone to care about Barclay's cold comfort. If his return to England is a mission of mercy consonant with his apparent spiritual transformation, it comes too late for Liz. His perfunctory gestures of sympathy notwithstanding, he has come primarily for Tucker. For the novel's title, action, and structure have long since made it clear that whatever moral resolution awaits Barclay must be worked out with Tucker.

If Liz's last words — "You and Rick have destroyed each other" — are true, then Barclay has come too late for Tucker as he came too late for her. Already driven to the edge of madness by Barclay's sadistic baiting, Tucker is reduced to a howling animal by his announcement that he will write the biography himself. Barclay delivers his crushing news during the last supper he arranges at the aptly named Random Club, where arbitrary slashing at one's fellowman is the preferred modus operandi. In the viciousness of his reversion to form, Barclay seems intent on vitiating the lesson of his radiant vision. Back home he learns of Liz's death and of the likelihood that his stigmata should be associated rather with the crucified thieves than with Christ. It is almost with relief that Barclay collapses back into the role he had once thought himself born to play — that of the predestinate damned: "Not for me the responsibility of goodness, the abject terror of being holy! For me the peace and security of knowing myself a thief!" If the novel were to end with this negative epiphany Barclay might well have damned himself. As it is, Golding contrives in the few remaining pages a denouement that renders the eschatological issue permanently inconclusive. After turning away the still imploring Tucker, apparently for the last time, Barclay inexplicably decides to "heal" him: "Suddenly the autobiography is no longer to be used to thwart Tucker, but will be handed over to him as a (literally) uncovenanted mercy, a mercy such as Barclay himself received in the form of the blessed vision and such as he still hopes for in the form of eternal annihilation of the self in death."[5] Thus the autobiography/novel that Barclay calls "a fair record of the various times the clown's trousers fell down" is that, and more. A prolonged act of expiation, it is also the potential salvation of the two paper men.

Having all but completed the manuscript he intends to hand over to Tucker, and built "the paperweight of a whole life" into an enormous bonfire, Barclay has consciously set his house — and his life — in order. Now "happy, quietly happy," a drinker who no longer needs a drink, he prepares to "disappear into comfort and security." Purged of intolerance and imbued with the "uncovenanted mercy" that drives him to give Tucker the "small sheaf of papers, all that is necessary," Barclay at last achieves real freedom. It is at this point that Tucker's bullet ends the life that in reality has just begun. The shot that puts an end to Barclay and the novel also suspends eschatological judgment. Does Barclay's moral about-face merit an eleventh-hour reprieve from the damnation the rest of his life seemed to earn? Or does it come — like his consolatory message for Liz — too late? Killed before he can give the manuscript to Tucker, Barclay can be judged solely on his intention, not on his act. By cutting Barclay off in the flush of his spiritually finest hour, thus making it impossible for him to backslide, Tucker may be the unwitting agent of his victim's salvation. But if salvation demands not only penitential thoughts but penitential deeds, then Tucker's is the ultimate revenge: he has tripped Barclay up at Heaven's gate.

In its deliberate inconclusiveness, what happens at the end of *The Paper Men* typifies Golding's endings. A representative protagonist, avatar of the depraved human condition yet child of a merciful God, plays out a scenario in which his salvation, if not imminent, is at least conceivable. Barclay's last thought is of "an uncovenanted mercy — a mercy by which those unsatisfactory phenomena, Wilfred Townsend Barclay and Richard Linbergh Tucker may be eternally destroyed." If Tucker's annihilating bullet signifies the mercy of eternal destruction, then Barclay is as saved as man can — and should — be. Life after death holds no more appeal for Golding than for Barclay:

No, I hope devoutly that there is no survival after death. I don't wish to live with myself for eternity. Eternity is far, far too long. I think any really merciful God would destroy painlessly, let us hope, creatures who've had seventy or eighty years of it.[6]

Nearing the end of his career, Golding is no more sanguine about the human condition than he was at the beginning. Men remain by and large Barclay's "unsatisfactory phenomena"; and the theme of *The Paper Men* recalls the theme of *Lord of the Flies*: "Grief, sheer grief, grief, grief, grief."[7]

Notes

Chapter 1: In Pursuit of Man:
The Dialectic of William Golding

1. William Golding, "Nobel Lecture," in *A Moving Target* (London: Faber and Faber, 1984), pp. 209–10.

2. William Golding, "Fable," in *The Hot Gates* (London: Faber and Faber, 1965), pp. 86–88.

3. William Golding, "The Ladder and the Tree," ibid., pp. 172–73.

4. Ibid., pp. 168–70.

5. Jack I. Biles, *Talk: Conversations with William Golding* (New York: Harcourt Brace Jovanovich, 1970), pp. 89–90.

6. William Golding, "My First Book," in *A Moving Target*, p. 147.

7. Ibid.

8. James R. Baker, "An Interview with William Golding," in *Twentieth-Century Literature*, 28:2 (Summer 1982), p. 131.

9. "William Golding Talks to John Carey, 10–11 July 1985," in *William Golding: The Man and His Books*, ed. John Carey (New York: Farrar Straus Giroux, 1986), p. 178.

10. Golding, *The Hot Gates*, pp. 85–101.

11. Baker, "William Golding," p. 145.

12. Ibid.

13. Ibid.

14. Ibid, p. 165.

15. Ibid., pp. 131–32.

16. William Golding, "Belief and Creativity," in *A Moving Target,* p. 199.

17. Baker, "William Golding," p. 134.

18. Golding, "Belief and Creativity," p. 201.

19. Baker, "William Golding," p. 169.

Chapter 2: Grief, Grief, Grief: *Lord of the Flies*

1. William Golding, the title essay in *A Moving Target,* p. 163.

2. Golding, "Fable," p. 88.

3. E. M. Forster, introduction, in William Golding, *Lord of the Flies* (New York: Coward-McCann, 1962), p. xiii.

4. Orson Welles, *Mr. Arkadin,* 1955. Welles, in the title role of a wealthy and powerful tycoon, relates this story at one of his sophisticated soirees. Written and directed by Welles, the film depicts Arkadin hunting down and killing former friends who might expose his shady past.

5. Golding, "Fable," pp. 97–98.

6. James R. Baker, *William Golding* (New York: St. Martin's Press, 1965), p. 13.

7. Jean-Paul Sartre, *The Flies,* in *"No Exit" and Three Other Plays,* tr. Stuart Gilbert (New York: Vintage, 1955), p. 51.

8. Biles, *Talk: Conversations with William Golding,* p. 106.

9. Bernard F. Dick, *William Golding* (New York: Twayne, 1967), p. 30.

10. Ibid., p. 31.

11. Golding, "A Moving Target," p. 163.

Chapter 3: Shadows of Forgotten Ancestors: *The Inheritors*

1. William Golding, "Digging for Pictures," in *The Hot Gates*, p. 62

2. Frank Kermode and William Golding, "The Meaning of it All," in *Books and Bookmen 5* (October 1959), p. 10.

3. Baker, "An Interview with William Golding," p. 150.

4. Ibid., p. 140.

5. Ibid.

6. Biles, *Talk: Conversations with William Golding*, p. 40.

7. Quoted in ibid., p. 106.

Chapter 4: A Double Dying: *Pincher Martin*

1. Baker, "An Interview with William Golding," p. 134.

2. Kermode and Golding, "The Meaning of it All," p. 10.

3. "Pincher Martin," *Radio Times*, 21 March 1958, p. 8.

4. Baker, "An Interview with William Golding," p. 132.

5. Ibid., p. 131.

6. Ibid., p. 144.

7. Golding, "The Ladder and the Tree," p. 173.

8. Bernard Dick, *William Golding* (Boston: Twayne, rev. ed., 1987), pp. 51–52.

9. Biles, *Talk: Conversations with William Golding*, p. 76.

10. Baker, "An Interview with William Golding," p. 143.

Chapter 5: Cosmic Chaos: *Free Fall*

1. Biles, *Talk: Conversations with William Golding*, p. 81.

2. Baker, "An Interview with William Golding," p. 133.

3. "Cosmic chaos," "patternlessness," "the natural chaos of existence" are terms used by Golding in a 1958 interview with Owen Webster. Quoted in James R. Baker, *William Golding*, pp. 54–57.

4. Quoted in Biles, *Talk: Conversations with William Golding*, p. 79.

5. Quoted in ibid., p. 75.

6. Arnold Johnston, *Of Earth and Darkness: The Novels of William Golding* (Columbia: University of Missouri Press, 1980), p. 60.

7. Baker, "An Interview with William Golding," p. 146.

8. Golding, "Belief and Creativity," p. 201.

Chapter 6: God's Visionary: *The Spire*

1. Baker, "An Interview with William Golding," p. 150.

2. Golding, "An Affection for Cathedrals," in *A Moving Target*, p. 17.

3. Baker, "An Interview with William Golding," p. 148.

4. Biles, *Talk: Conversations with William Golding*, pp. 98–100.

5. Herbert Mitgang, "William Golding's World," in the *New York Times Book Review* (November 2, 1980), p. 47.

6. Baker, "An Interview with William Golding," p. 150.

Chapter 7: Between the Acts: *The Pyramid* and *The Scorpion God: Three Short Novels*

1. Golding, *A Moving Target*, p. 82.

2. Ibid., p. 67.

3. Baker, "An Interview with William Golding," p. 160.

4. Ibid., p. 153.

5. Ibid., p. 155.

6. Golding, "The Ladder and the Tree," p. 168.

7. Quoted in Don Crompton, *A View from the Spire: William Golding's Later Novels,* edited and completed by Julia Briggs (Oxford: Blackwell, 1985), pp. 61–62.

8. Baker, "An Interview with William Golding," p. 158. Golding claims that this view of the Egyptians, which he attributes to Herodotus, inspired "The Scorpion God." Still, Golding's assertion that "I had the Egyptology up my sleeve all the time" indicates its relevance to *The Pyramid* as well.

9. Baker, "An Interview with William Golding," p. 154.

10. Ibid., pp. 158–60.

11. James Gindin, *William Golding* (New York: St. Martin's Press, 1988), p. 63.

12. Baker, "An Interview with William Golding," p. 160.

Chapter 8: Fire Sermon: *Darkness Visible*

1. Biles, *Talk: Conversations with William Golding,* pp. 61–63.

2. Golding, "Fable," pp. 86–87.

3. Golding, *A Moving Target,* p. 168.

4. Golding, *The Hot Gates,* pp. 29–30.

Chapter 9: Sentimental Journey: *The Sea Trilogy*

1. Baker, "An Interview with William Golding," p. 163.

2. Ibid., p. 160.

3. Quoted in Mark Kinkead-Weekes and Ian Gregor, *William Golding: A Critical Study* (London: Faber and Faber, 1984), p. 269.

4. Baker, "An Interview with William Golding," p. 164.

5. Ibid.

6. Ibid., p. 160.

7. Ibid., p. 162.

8. Ibid.

9. Gindin, *William Golding*, p. 77.

Chapter 10: Writing and Its Discontents: *The Paper Men*

1. See S. J. Boyd, *The Novels of William Golding* (Sussex: Harvester Press; and New York: St. Martin's Press, 1988), p. 199.

2. Leon Edel and Lyall H. Powers, eds., *The Complete Notebooks of Henry James* (Oxford: Oxford University Press, 1987), p. 34.

3. Crompton, *A View from the Spire*, pp. 172, 176.

4. Boyd, *The Novels of William Golding*, p. 191.

5. Crompton, *A View from the Spire*, pp. 182–183.

6. Baker, "An Interview with William Golding," p. 143.

7. Golding, "A Moving Target," p. 163.

Bibliography

Works by William Golding
(Fiction unless otherwise noted)

Poems. London: Macmillan & Co., 1934. Reprint. New York: Macmillan Co. 1935.

Lord of the Flies. London: Faber & Faber, 1954. Reprint. New York: Coward-McCann, 1955.

The Inheritors. London: Faber & Faber, 1955. Reprint. New York: Harcourt, Brace & World, 1962.

Pincher Martin. London: Faber & Faber, 1956. Reprint. *The Two Deaths of Christopher Martin.* New York: Harcourt, Brace & World, 1957.

The Brass Butterfly. London: Faber & Faber, 1958. Play.

Free Fall. London: Faber & Faber, 1959. Reprint. New York: Harcourt, Brace & World, 1962.

The Spire. London: Faber & Faber, 1964. Reprint. New York: Harcourt, Brace & World, 1964.

The Hot Gates and Other Occasional Pieces. London: Faber & Faber, 1965. Reprint. New York: Harcourt, Brace & World, 1966. Essays.

The Pyramid. London: Faber & Faber, 1967. Reprint. New York: Harcourt, Brace & World, 1967.

The Scorpion God: Three Short Novels. London: Faber & Faber, 1971. Reprint. New York: Harcourt Brace Jovanovich, 1972.

Darkness Visible. London: Faber & Faber, 1979. Reprint. New York: Farrar, Straus & Giroux, 1979.

Rites of Passage. London: Faber & Faber, 1980. Reprint. New York: Farrar, Straus & Giroux, 1980.

A Moving Target. London: Faber & Faber, 1982. Reprint. New York: Farrar, Straus & Giroux, 1983. Essays.

The Paper Men. London: Faber & Faber, 1984. Reprint. New York: Farrar, Straus & Giroux, 1984.

An Egyptian Journal. London: Faber & Faber, 1985. Travel

Close Quarters. London: Faber & Faber, 1987. Reprint. New York: Farrar, Straus & Giroux, 1987.

Fire down Below. London: Faber & Faber, 1989. Reprint. New York: Farrar, Straus & Giroux, 1989.

Selected Books and Articles on William Golding

Babb, Howard S. *The Novels of William Golding*. Columbus: Ohio State University Press, 1970.

Baker, James R. *William Golding: A Critical Study*. New York: St. Martin's Press, 1965.

———, ed. *Critical Essays on William Golding*. Boston: G. K. Hall, 1988.

Biles, Jack. *Talk: Conversations with William Golding*. New York: Harcourt Brace Jovanovich, 1970.

Biles, Jack, and Robert Evans, eds. *William Golding: Some Critical Considerations*. Lexington: University of Kentucky Press, 1978.

Boyd, S. J. *The Novels of William Golding*. Sussex: Harvester Press, 1988. New York: St. Martin's Press, 1988.

Carey, John, ed. *William Golding: The Man and His Books*. New York: Farrar, Straus & Giroux, 1987.

Crompton, Don. *A View from the Spire: William Golding's Later Novels*. Edited and completed by Julia Briggs. New York: Blackwell, 1985.

Dick, Bernard F. *William Golding*. Revised Edition. Boston: Twayne Publishers, 1987.

Gindin, James. *William Golding*. New York: St. Martin's Press, 1988.

Gregor, Ian, and Mark Kinkead-Weekes. *William Golding: A Critical Study*. Revised Edition. London: Faber & Faber, 1984.

Hynes, Samuel. *William Golding*. 2nd Edition. New York: Columbia University Press, 1968.

Kermode, Frank, and William Golding. "The Meaning of It All." *Books and Bookmen 5* (October 1959): 9–10.

Oldsey, Bernard S., and Stanley Weintraub. *The Art of William Golding*. New York: Harcourt, Brace & World, 1965.

Peter, John. "The Fables of William Golding." *Kenyon Review* 19 (Autumn 1957): 577–92.

Sabbarao, V. V. *William Golding: A Study*. New York: Envoy Press, 1987.

Tiger, Virginia. *William Golding: The Dark Fields of Discovery*. London: Edward Arnold, 1970.

Twentieth Century Literature 28 (Summer 1982). Special Golding issue.

Index